RICHARD CRAZE AND RONI JAY

THE
TAO
OF FOOD

A GODSFIELD BOOK

RICHARD CRAZE AND RONI JAY

THE TAO OF FOOD

A GODSFIELD BOOK

Library of Congress Cataloging-in-Publication Data Available

10 9 8 7 6 5 4 3 2 1

Published in 1999 by Sterling Publishing Company, Inc.
387 Park Avenue South, New York, N.Y. 10016

DESIGNED FOR GODSFIELD PRESS BY
THE BRIDGEWATER BOOK COMPANY LTD.

Picture Research Lynda Marshall
Illustrations Jane Hadfield
Studio Photography Walter Gardiner Photographers

Distributed in Canada by Sterling Publishing
c/o Canadian Manda Group, One Atlantic Avenue, Suite 105
Toronto, Ontario, Canada M6K 3E7
Distributed in Australia by Capricorn Link (Australia) Pty Ltd
P. O. Box 6651, Baulkham Hills Business Centre, NSW 2153, Australia

Printed in Hong Kong

Sterling ISBN 0-8069-7075-8

PICTURE CREDITS
(a = above)
Elizabeth Whiting & Associates pp 27, 35, 37, 40, 46, 49, 51
e. t. archive pp 8, 9a, 44, 54
Image Bank pp 2, 6, 11, 13, 18a, 25a, 28–29, 36, 38, 41, 53, 64, 95

CONTENTS

Introduction

Food provides the energy we need to function physically, to enjoy ourselves, and to experience life in full: as the maxim goes, we are what we eat. What about the quality of the food we eat, and the way it is cooked and prepared? There is an old Chinese saying that summarizes the Taoist approach to diet: "hasty food, hasty energy." In the modern world it is easy to forget the importance of a healthy, balanced diet; the current tendency in the West is toward busy lifestyles, fast foods, and limited diets. Is this the right way to nourish ourselves?

The Tao of Food is a book for people who want to learn how to prepare food and cook in a more leisurely and pleasurable way at the same time as improving their health and boosting their energy. It is written for those who realize and appreciate that what we eat defines our health and well-being; if we rush everything, especially our food, our lives will fly by without our even noticing it, let alone enjoying it. And good health is so much more than avoiding disease and illness; it is about living life to the full and appreciating all that we have been given.

In *The Tao of Food* we will look at ways of improving our diet according to the principles of Taoist philosophy. We will examine the five element theory – the Chinese understanding of warming and cooling foods and their significance in the pursuit of harmony – and the principles of *yin* and *yang*; we will look at what sort of food will benefit us, where and how to buy it, how to prepare it, and the significance of the taste, texture, and symbolism of food; and we will consider ways of improving the way we cook, what sort of utensils and fuel we use, and how to present and serve the final dish. We shall also look at karma.

Chinese medicine goes back as far as 2000 B.C. and its basic principles were established during a time when people were living close to nature and the seasons. Everything was much simpler. The ancient Taoists of China considered a healthy diet as crucial to fulfillment; they classed it as one of the five sacred tools of life – the others being medicine, sex, good breathing, and longevity – all of which they believed to be interconnected. Without good food, they advised, we cannot expect our breathing to be right. Without good breathing we cannot eat properly or enjoy sex. Without eating healing foods our health suffers and our longevity is curtailed.

The Taoist philosophy is said to originate in ancient China.

THE TAOIST APPROACH

*Before we can look at what we eat and how
it affects us, we need to look at what Taoism
means and how it came about.*

WE ARE WHAT WE EAT

Taosim is an ancient Chinese philosophy that was originally taught in texts – the most famous being the *Tao te ching* ("the way of change") thought to be written in the fourth century B.C. and based on the teachings of Lao Tzu, a Chinese philosopher who flourished in the sixth century B.C. Although the book appeared 300 years after his death, legend has it that when Lao Tzu was 96, he chose to leave China but before he departed he was asked to write down his philosophy of life. In only one evening he wrote about 81 verses that expressed his beliefs concerning existence. Barely 30 pages long, the *Tao te ching* has become one of the most important books in Chinese philosophy. Though it uses few words (just over 5,000), its message is of such profound significance that scholars have continued to debate its meaning for over 3,000 years.

However, the message in the *Tao te ching* is not obscure – it is there for anyone to decipher according to their understanding of the text. In brief, it says that there is a way – the Way (*Tao* means "way" or "path"). The Way is constant, even if everything else is in flux, and if we follow the Way we will have a long and enjoyable life; if we don't follow it we encounter problems, ill health, and unhappiness. There are no rules, no precepts, and no religious practice involved with the Tao: the aim is to enjoy life and effortlessly accept the world around us.

If we try to change the Tao and impose our own rules or thoughts upon it we will be frustrated in our efforts. The *Tao te ching* says that no matter what we do the sun will come up and new life will emerge from old. Yet, within the unchanging *Tao* there is constant change. We need to accept that change and adjust accordingly. In the winter we need to wear warmer clothes and eat warmer food; in the summer we can wear lighter clothes and eat cooler food. This simplicity is at the heart of Taoism.

Taken together, the Taoist principles – laid down over 3,000 years ago – cover all aspects of what and how we eat, and they significantly improve our well-being without our having to adopt or adhere to any rigid disciplines or complicated diets. The Taoist principles are based on sound common sense and simplicity. If we incorporate them into our daily lives we can improve our health, sex, breathing, and longevity, as well as enjoy food again in a new and invigorating way.

Lao Tzu, was a minor government official, and probably a record-keeper, in China. In the last years of his life he recorded his personal philosophy, which formed the basis of Taoism.

"There is nothing hidden between Heaven and Earth"

A fresh peach, warm from the sun and recently picked, embodies the Taoist principle of freshness, simplicity, and the natural way.

The Symbol of the Peach

The Taoists sought immortality through everlasting longevity, and they used the symbol of a peach *(Prunus persica)* to remind them of this aim. What could be better for you than a fresh peach just plucked from the tree? It is still warm from the sun, full of juice and live *ch'i* energy.

When you follow the Taoist approach to cooking and eating, it is worth bearing in mind the symbol of the peach; then, when you are unsure of the goodness of any food, all you have to do is ask yourself whether it compares with a fresh peach. Has it been recently harvested? Is it still full of goodness and warmth from the sun?

Ch'i: Universal Energy

The Taoists said that first there was heaven, which represents the spirit. From heaven, matter or earth was created, and from the earth we were made to enjoy the creation. Between heaven and earth there flows constant energy – *ch'i*. This universal energy is in all things, including us. We are kept alive by *ch'i* energy, and everything that we eat contains *ch'i* energy.

Processed and refined foods lack the energy that fresh foods provide; instead they fill us with chemicals and toxins that block energy as it flows around the body.

When we digest our food we generate new, fresh energy that revitalizes us and keeps us alive. If we eat "dead" food, which lacks *ch'i*, we will feel sluggish and lethargic. Dead food is that which has passed its "sell-by" date in the natural world: vegetables that have been left too long and have begun to decompose; meat that has been frozen for a long time or has begun to spoil; milk that has been taken from a cow and processed so that it has lost its freshness; fruit that has not been picked from a tree while it is still still warm from the sun.

If the dead energy in dead food is allowed to stagnate too much it could actually poison us with harmful *ch'i*, the result of the energy becoming unstable and destructive. In this state it is better to bury it and allow that energy to be reabsorbed back into the earth rather than for us to eat it.

One method of assessing the energy in your food is to leave a sample out overnight. Will you still want to eat it in the morning? Refined and processed foods spoil very quickly and will not be appetizing after a night out on the kitchen table. According to Taoist principles, the closer food is to its natural state, and the less sophisticated, processed, and refined it is, then the more goodness and nourishment it contains.

The Cycle of *Ch'i*

The Way of *ch'i*, the Tao of *ch'i*, is constant movement and transformation. When we digest the food, the *ch'i* it contains is changed into energy to sustain us and give us life. In living, we use that energy to work and to take pleasure. Work and pleasure both create *ch'i* and use *ch'i* in a constant cycle of energy consumption and generation. Most Chinese medicine is traditionally based on the idea that *ch'i* energy moves within our bodies along invisible pathways called meridians. If the meridians become blocked or the *ch'i* energy becomes sluggish or stagnant, or flows too fast, we suffer ill health. By gently stimulating certain points along these meridians a Chinese medical practitioner can free the energy and restore health. This stimulation is done by applying gentle pressure on the specific meridian points (acupressure), or by inserting needles at these points to regulate energy flow (acupuncture).

Chinese doctors often recommend acupuncture to restore vital ch'i *energy to the body. Acupuncture ensures that the meridians – or energy lines – around the body are fully functional.*

The Holistic Approach

The holistic approach takes into account a person's mind as well as the body. In fact holistic practitioners believe that all aspects of a person's lifestyle including work, relationships, and daily habits are linked to health. "Holistic" is a word used by many communities and individuals; it basically means that all the aspects of life are relevant and interconnected – any imbalances are bound to contribute to illness and unhappiness.

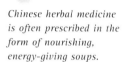

Chinese herbal medicine is often prescribed in the form of nourishing, energy-giving soups.

Preventative Medicine

Chinese medicine follows the holistic principle and as a result it advocates preventative rather than curative or symptomatic treatment. If you are ill it is because something has gone wrong with your energy flow and the practitioner will try to put it right by prescribing herbs and applying acupuncture or acupressure. However, he or she will also advise you on your diet and lifestyle. By eating according to the Taoist principles, the flow of energy can be both maintained and kept vigorous; thus ill health can be kept at bay.

Eating Medicine

Chinese doctors also use herbal medicine, which they believe restores the balance of the *ch'i* energy by boosting the amount and type of energy available. If you've been eating poorly, then they will boost your entire system with concentrated energy provided by a carefully selected combination of herbs. They call this practice "eating medicine," because many of the herbs are given in the form of tasty, nourishing soup.

Chinese medicine works in response to the Taoist philosophy that there is a Way and if we deflect from that Way our life suffers through ill health or unhappiness. There is a need for good, free-flowing energy within our bodies and if that energy is corrupted we become ill. The flow of energy needs to be vigorous to maintain good health; it can be improved and maintained by changing what we eat.

Although Chinese doctors study for years before prescribing herbal remedies, anyone can take the basic premise of Chinese medicine and apply it to his or her daily life. In China there is a long tradition of the home use of herbs that can be added to salads; but more often they are cooked in the form of fresh soups – rich in vitamins and minerals.

"Health is not everything; without health, 'though, everything is worth nothing"

Regular exercise and lots of fresh air will complement a healthy, Taoist diet.

YIN AND *YANG*

To take the Taoist approach to eating one step further, we must next look at the different types of *ch'i* that food contains. As we have seen, the Taoists believe that in the beginning was heaven (representing spirit and light), and, later, all matter (earth and dark) was created from heaven. Between the two there is a constant interchange of *ch'i* energy. The spirit (light) part of energy is called *yang* and it is considered to be the masculine force in the universe. The matter (dark) part of energy is called *yin* and is the feminine force in the universe. Yet nothing ever consists entirely of *yin* or *yang*. If you look at a *yin/yang* symbol you will see a dot of light *yang* in the dark swirl of *yin*, and a dark spot of *yin* in the light swirl of *yang*. Within each there is always the seed of the other, ready to change and grow, to transform into its opposite.

THE QUALITIES OF YIN AND YANG

Yin: inner, down, north, negative, passive, receptive, night, cold, soft, wet, winter, shadow, interior, moist, retiring, lingering, larger.

Yang: outer, up, south, sky, positive, active, day, heat, dry, summer, sunshine, surface, powerful, quick, smaller.

Yin and Yang Foods

The notion that foods can be defined as predominantly *yin* or *yang* is very old, but it is important to remember that in a Taoist approach to cooking and food we seek to find a balance. If you eat predominantly *yin* foods your body will be capable of producing only *yin* energy – darker, slower-moving, and colder. If you eat predominantly *yang* foods you will produce only *yang* energy – faster, hotter, and much more energetic. During certain times, such as illness or when recovering from major surgery, you may well need to eat only one type either to restore the energy balance of your body or to shift an energy blockage.

Which is Which?

Without classifying every type of food, it might be helpful to remember certain rules that determine the type of energy that a certain food produces:

- if it grows in the air and sunshine it is probably *yang*;
- if it grows in the earth or darkness it is probably *yin*;
- if it is salty it is *yang*; if it is sweet it is *yin*;
- if it is lean it is *yang*; if it is fatty it is *yin*;
- if it is rich in sodium it is *yang*;
- if it is rich in potassium it is *yin*.

Most meat, for example, is *yang*, but if you choose fatty cuts then they have some *yin* in them. If you choose fish, the smaller, faster-moving fish are more *yang* while the larger, slower-moving fish are more *yin*.

Yang foods will make you feel full up and warm, whereas *yin* foods will leave you feeling cooler and less full. Fruit, which you might think of as *yang,* is actually *yin* because it grows within its own darkness, it is wet and moist, and it leaves you feeling lighter, less full, and cooler. A lean red steak, on the other hand, is dryer, much higher in potassium, and fills and warms you up.

You might think that you could achieve balance by eating very *yang* foods, such as eggs, red meat, poultry, and fish, at the same time as eating very *yin* foods, such as sugar, soft fruit, nuts, and soft full-fat cheeses, but this isn't the case. Your stomach would find it very hard to process such extremes of energy and would react quite badly. The balance should be achieved by eating foods that themselves are in balance, containing a healthy mix of both *yin* and *yang.*

"Where-so-ever you go, go with all your heart"

Balanced Foods

LIMA BEANS

The foods that contain a good balance of both *yin* and *yang* energy are grains, seeds, and pulses. These have grown inside a dark *yin* environment in the flesh of the fruit or vegetable even though the fruit or vegetable itself has been exposed to the sunshine. Seeds, grains, and pulses aren't too full of either sodium or potassium and they provide healthy energy without making too many demands on the digestive system.

Rice, which we will deal with in some detail a little later (see page 28), serves as a good example of a *yin* and *yang* food. It is almost perfectly placed between the two extremes and provides both types of energy. Some people may consider rice to be bland or boring, this is because they aren't getting the heavily *yin* or heavily *yang* "hit" that their bodies have come to expect.

RED LENTILS

If food is big in size, soft, wet, and cool (such as a melon), it is more *yin*. If the food is smaller, hard, dry, spicy, or needs heating up (such as meat), then it is more *yang*. Vegetables are predominantly *yin* but root vegetables are nicely balanced. Leafy salad foods are quite *yin* because they grow in the earth, and the larger the seeds the more *yin* they are. Cheese is quite well-balanced, but hard, salty cheeses are more *yang*, and soft, fatty cheeses more *yin*. Cream, yogurt, and milk are quite *yin* and the fattier they are the more *yin* they are. Fruit is basically *yin*, especially the larger, wetter fruits, although harder fruit, such as hard apples, contain a better balance of *yang*.

BLACK BEANS

YELLOW SPLIT PEAS

Most foods can be classified as predominantly yin *or predominantly* yang *foods. Some foods, however, such as beans, grains, and pulses provide a good balance between the two extremes.*

RICE

MELON

LEAFY SALAD VEGETABLES

APPLE

MEAT

HARD CHEESE

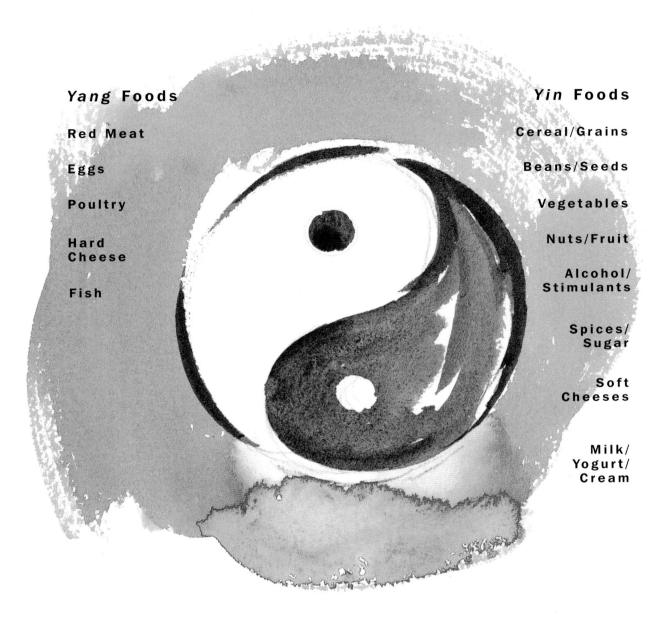

Yang Foods

Red Meat

Eggs

Poultry

Hard Cheese

Fish

Yin Foods

Cereal/Grains

Beans/Seeds

Vegetables

Nuts/Fruit

Alcohol/Stimulants

Spices/Sugar

Soft Cheeses

Milk/Yogurt/Cream

This yin/yang diagram provides an easy reminder of which foods fall into which category. When you follow recipes or make up your own dishes, you will be able to combine food to suit a Taoist diet.

Creating Inner *Feng Shui*

Feng shui (literally "wind and water") is the ancient Eastern art of arranging your environment and landscape to make best use of the *ch'i* flowing into your life. *Ch'i* flows through all things and across all landscapes, and it brings with it energy and vitality. It also picks up the residue of anything it has recently passed over or through. Thus, if you live facing an abattoir or cemetery, the *ch'i* entering your home will be tainted by the pain and loss of that place and may affect you adversely. If you live facing a beautiful view of open country, woods, streams, and green fields, then the *ch'i* entering your home will be revitalized and healthy and will, in turn, bring you new vitality and health.

Developments of the modern world have affected the balance of ch'i in our lives. Expressways, for example, create negative ch'i and may affect crops if they are growing nearby.

Crops grown next to an expressway will not only contain increased quantities of poisonous lead from fuel fumes, but their *ch'i* will also be adversely affected, so the life they bring when they are eaten will be stagnant and corrupt. Crops grown in tranquil, clean, harmonious fields will impart a fresh *ch'i*, which can only do you good.

Although there is no such thing as set rules for what and how we eat and cook the Taoist way, certain guidelines, which are all based on sound common sense, go a long way toward creating inner *feng shui*.

Seasonal Food

In the summer, eat cooler foods, such as salads, that need less cooking. This will increase your internal *yin*, which will help combat the external *yang* heat generated by sunshine. In the winter, eat warmer *yang* food, such as stews and casseroles, which will renew the much-needed inner *yang* warmth that is being cooled by the *yin* weather conditions. In the spring, eat more vegetables, which will restore your internal balance of *yin* and *yang*. In the fall, begin to eat more fruit and nuts in preparation for the cold *yin* winter.

Life Changes

When we are young we are more *yang*, and as we grow older we become more *yin*. Because small children are very *yang* they hanker after very sweet *yin* foods to combat their *yang* energy. Older people have become more *yin* and are attracted to very *yang* foods to try to warm them internally. If we lead very energetic lives we need more *yang* food to provide the energy; if we are sedentary we need less *yang* and more *yin* foods.

A Healthy Balance

We should eat foods that are healthily balanced between *yin* and *yang*; any foods that are predominantly one or the other should be treated with some caution unless you feel that your system can handle them. A little red meat (considered very *yang*) and a little sugar (considered very *yin*) on occasion is not going to harm anyone. If, however, the diet consists only of extreme types of food, our health will be affected. We all know the type of person who eat heavily *yin* or heavily *yang* diets: florid-faced *yang* meat-eaters with high blood pressure and clogged arteries; overweight, sweet-dependent *yin* types with pale skin and no vital energy.

"A closed mind is like a closed book; just a block of wood"

Try to eat some grains every day – in your cereal perhaps. Grains are a good example of a food that strikes a healthy balance between yin *and* yang.

Tao Tips for a Daily Diet

We should aim to eat some whole grains every day to restore and maintain balance. This means including oats, rice, barley, wholewheat spaghetti, pasta, and noodles in our daily diet. We should also try to eat some beans and nuts every day, as well as seeds of some kind. These foods contain a good balance of *yin* and *yang* and are nutritious and healthy.

Cutting out sugar in its refined form isn't as hard as you might think. It can be replaced, but alternatives such as honey and molasses are also highly *yin*. It is better simply to retrain your palate to avoid sweet foods. Natural foods don't need sweetening.

Reducing our consumption of *yang* foods, such as red meat, will mean switching to poultry and fish. We can also balance *yang* foods by serving them with *yin* sauces flavored with lemon, horseradish, mustard, root ginger, and spices.

Eat Locally

Unless you live in the tropics you don't really need too many tropical foods, especially the very *yin* fruits such as pineapples, figs, dates, and chilis. These are all very *yin* because it is necessary to combat the heat of the *yang* tropical climate – not so essential if you live in a temperate region. Obviously, if the weather gets very hot, then cooling *yin* fruits are the best foods you can eat to combat the heat. Likewise, in very cold weather conditions, it is beneficial to eat very warming *yang* foods, such as meat stews and casseroles.

Tropical fruits suit their climate; they are very yin *and help cool the body in extreme heat. Root vegetables are well-balanced between* yin *and* yang; *they are ideal for a country where the climate is mixed.*

The Tao of Dairy Foods

When a calf is born its first few months are spent growing. Cow's milk is designed to be very rich in protein and calcium to aid growth. Human milk, on the other hand, is very rich in carbohydrates to feed the enormous growth in brain size that human children undergo in their first few months of life. The two are quite different and shouldn't be confused. We need a lot of milk when we are very young but only a moderate amount as we get older. Milk is a natural and vital resource that we should make good use of, but as adults our intake of dairy foods should not be too high.

ASPARAGUS

GINSENG

CINNAMON

GARLIC

HEALING FOODS

Asparagus, garlic, cinnamon, and ginseng are all considered by Taoists to have healing properties: asparagus aids resistance against colds; garlic is good for the blood; cinnamon combats pain from arthritis; and ginseng enhances vital energy.

When we are in good health and free from stress we can eat what we want and our bodies can process it easily. However, if we are ill or suffering from stress, then our bodies will be unable to tolerate any foods that are too *yang* or too *yin*. The Taoists consider healing foods to be those that restore the balance between *yin* and *yang*: if we are feverish, then we need cooling *yin* foods; if we are cold and shivery, then we need hot *yang* food to return the body to its usual temperature.

Convalescents and those recovering from surgery or major illness have their own special dietary requirements. At these times, the digestive system should not be overloaded, so softer, more moist food should be eaten to relieve the stomach of any effort. The Taoists rely on healing soups to aid recovery from illness, and they consider them to be an essential part of our daily diet to help maintain health.

Food for the Body

The Taoists also believe that certain foods are helpful in curing certain illnesses. For instance, garlic is thought to keep the blood *ch'i* fresh; ginseng tones the whole system and provides abundant energy; cinnamon will relieve the pain in arthritic joints and ease period pains; asparagus helps combat the onset of winter colds and coughs; chrysanthemum flowers can help migraine sufferers prevent recurring attacks; peppermint strengthens the lungs; dandelion will restore stagnating stomach *ch'i* (which can cause ulcers); and fresh ginger will warm excessive cold and restore stagnant *ch'i*. There are many more foods that could be mentioned; all of them universally known for their curative powers (as well as their preventative properties).

CHRYSANTHEMUM
FLOWERS

FRESH GINGER

Food for Thought

Healing foods can also be eaten to change mental attitudes: if we
lack confidence and depend too much on others to support us, we
may need to eat more *yang* foods to give us mental strength. If
we are overly assertive, aggressive, and stubborn we may need to
eat more *yin* foods. *Yang* foods will make us hotter and more
volatile; *yin* foods will have a pacifying effect. *Yang* foods will
speed up the system while *yin* foods will slow us down.

Taoists believe that the more rigid our thinking patterns, the
more *yang* we are and in need of *yin* food to restore our
equilibrium. The looser our thinking and the more disorganized,
lazy, and apathetic we are, the more *yin* we have become; in this
instance we need *yang* food to restore our vital energy. Only you
can judge which food type you need. Remember the aim is to
achieve harmony and balance – there will always be a time for
energy, effort, and speed (*yang*) and also a time for pro-
crastination, relaxation, and daydreaming (*yin*). It is only when
we are predominantly one or the other that problems are caused.

Emotional Foods

Our emotions are also affected by what we eat. Overly *yang* foods
produce tension, which can cause aggression and anger because
the energy being created in our bodies is very intense. Overly *yin*
foods, which generate energy higher up in the body, can be the
cause of fear, anxiety, and emotional instability.

Sudden mood swings are caused by a *yang* surfeit. Outbursts of
crying and depression are caused by a *yin* surfeit. By restoring the
balance we can be in harmony both emotionally and mentally.
Our sense of humor returns and we feel bright and optimistic –
absolutely nothing can get in our way!

*Chrysanthemum flowers
and fresh ginger can be
used effectively in our
diets to combat illness:
chrysanthemum flowers
offer relief to migraine
sufferers and fresh
ginger is warming.*

"Soaring birds,
swimming fish,
flowing waters,
passing clouds
are the wheel of
essential nature
turning"

THE FIVE ELEMENTS

As well as defining energy as either *yin* or *yang*, the Taoists also break it down into five different types: fire, wood, earth, metal, and water. *Yang* energy is represented by fire which gives heat, light, and speed. *Yin* energy is represented by water which gives moisture, coolness, and depth. Earth is placed at the center with a perfect balance of both *yin* and *yang*. Wood is known as the lesser *yang* because it is mostly *yang* but with some *yin*. Metal is known as the lesser *yin* because it is mostly *yin* with some *yang*.

Discovering your Element

The five types of energy also equate to five different types of people. Knowing which type you are can help you decide on your diet. For instance, fire types are very *yang* and need lots of *yin* food to quell the heat. Water types are very *yin* and need lots of *yang* food to warm them up. Wood types need less *yin* food than fire types but should still go for a predominantly *yin* diet. Metal types need less *yang* food than water types but should still go for a predominantly *yang* diet. Earth types are well-balanced and should seek well-balanced *yin/yang* food.

It is easy to find out your elemental profile; all you need to know is your year of birth, because the element cycle is a repeating pattern. As you can see from the chart below, if you were born in 1962 this would make you a *yang* water type; born in 1958 and you'd be a *yang* earth; 1927 a *yin* fire. You will notice that odd numbers are *yin* and even numbers are *yang*, and there are five pairs of two years – the two metal years (0, 1), the two water years (2, 3), the two wood years (4, 5), the two fire years (6, 7), and the two earth years (8, 9).

Year	0	1	2	3	4	5	6	7	8	9
Element	Yang metal	Yin metal	Yang water	Yin water	Yang wood	Yin wood	Yang fire	Yin fire	Yang earth	Yin earth

Elemental Types

The Taoists also consider that each of these five elements goes toward making up our personality. No one is entirely just one of the five. Ideally we should be a perfect balance of all five, and through good cooking and eating we can redress any imbalance there may be.

FIRE

Fire types love excitement and crave new sensations. They are quick, active people who like to be busy, successful, and energetic. They may suffer from high blood pressure and stress, and they get exhausted easily.

WOOD

Wood types are very physically active and creative. They tend to be very supple and are quick, decisive people. They may suffer from headaches and migraines and are prone to muscular aches and strains.

WATER

Water people are intelligent and thoughtful. They are emotionally reserved and very imaginative. They may suffer from a lack of energy, low libido, and back problems.

METAL

Metal types are organized. They like to be in control and set very high standards for themselves and others. They may suffer from stiff joints, dry skin, and poor circulation.

EARTH

Earth types are garrulous and social. They enjoy good food and entertaining. They may suffer from fluid retention and digestive problems.

"Helping" and "Hindering"

Each of these five elements "helps" or "hinders" the others. For instance, water would be considered to help wood but to hinder fire. This is obvious, because anything growing needs water, but water extinguishes fire.

- Fire helps earth. Earth helps metal. Metal helps water. Water helps wood. Wood helps fire.
- Fire hinders metal. Metal hinders wood. Wood hinders earth. Earth hinders water. Water hinders fire.

All this is important to Taoist cooking because you need to know what helps and hinders. We need to cook in metal pots and use fire to cook with. We need the wood to fuel the fire and the earth to grow the food. Together all these elements can work to our benefit or work in opposition to our detriment.

A TAOIST MNEMONIC

To make the sequence easier to remember, the Taoists think of it like this: a burning wood fire melts the earth to produce metal, which is made into a bucket to carry water, but a burning wood fire would reduce metal to a molten mass and thus hinder it; a metal ax would hinder wood by chopping it down; wood hinders the earth by drawing all its nourishment from it; the earth hinders water by turning it to mud; and water hinders fire by extinguishing it.

Simplicity in Moderation

Taoism is about simplicity. A plain wood fire is simple, efficient, and harmonious, but a microwave oven, while still doing the cooking, is not in the spirit of Taoism; it is too complex and far too removed from nature and thus simplicity. An iron pot is simple and well made, but modern nonstick surfaces in pans are not in the spirit of Taoism; they are too complex and use too many resources and materials.

The spirit of Taoism, however, is not about denial or a back-to-nature philosophy; it is based on sound common sense. You should use what is available but if you have a choice, take the simplest path.

In the ideal Taoist kitchen, your cooking fire would be made from logs culled from trees that you have chopped yourself, or that your ancestors have planted.

THE SYMBOLISM OF FOOD

We looked earlier at the peach, the Taoist symbol for longevity. Rice is also very significant in Taoism. In particular, grains of rice are an extremely important part of Taoist symbolism. The Chinese calligraphy for *ch'i* energy and rice are virtually identical.

Grains of rice are seen as representing all the knowledge about Taoism; they contain *yin* and *yang*, the five elements, and the notion of heaven and earth. The rice itself is the *yin* and *yang* – as it is cooked, the rice represents matter or earth, while the steam is spirit or heaven. The rice is earth cooked in a metal pot in water over fire with wood. What could be more complete?

In the early days, rice was cooked in open earthenware pots, but as metal became more common, metal pans with lids came into fashion. When rice is steamed in a metal pan with a lid, the steam condenses on the underside of the lid – thus water is produced. This is another reason why the Taoists say that the element of metal "helps" water.

Rice is part of the staple diet in China and provides a good balance of yin *and* yang.

Growing Rice

The way rice is grown is also very symbolic of the entire Taoist tradition. Rice grows from earth in water. It is cut and harvested with metal tools with wooden handles. The image of the peasant farmers harvesting their own rice crop is a powerful symbol of work, self-sufficiency, simplicity, and harmony with the landscape – all central Taoist tenets. We could learn a lot from this image about being more in rhythm with nature.

A Useful Reminder

The Taoists say, "in a grain of rice, everything." This symbolism not only represents the entirety of Taoist teaching but is also a useful reminder of what we are trying to achieve with *The Tao of Food*: a healthy balance of both *yin* and *yang* as well as a beneficial combination of the five elements. The single grain of rice also represents *ch'i*. The stomach is the cooking pot, and the digestive system the fire. The *ch'i* energy, or steam, rises from the "cooked" food to the lungs, which are known as "heaven's gate."

"Enjoy yourself. It's later than you think"

COLOR, TASTE, AND TEXTURE

How food looks is very important. If you only ever eat one type of food you will starve yourself visually as well as physically. Food should look good, taste good, and be good for you. If we eat only soft *yin* foods our teeth will suffer, just as they will if we eat only excessively hard *yang* foods. As in all aspects of Taoist cooking, we need to find the right balance.

The Color of Food

The philosophy behind the definition of foods as *yin* or *yang* also applies to the colors of food, which can serve as a useful indication as to whether food is *yin* or *yang*:

- yin food, predominantly from plants, are soft and cooling. The cool colors, such as violet and blue, are also yin.
- yang food, predominantly from the animal world, are hard and warming. The warm colors, such as red and orange, are also yang.
- Midway between the two are the colors and foods that are a good balance, such as the yellows and greens.

If we only choose food that is red in color – *yang* food – we will suffer from excess internal heat that can make us bottle up our emotions and become stressed and aggressive. If we choose only soft, dark, *yin* food we will suffer from excess internal cold which will make us overemotional and weak.

Eat your Greens

Milky yang *clouds in your* yin *black coffee will produce a satisfying balance between the two principles.*

If we choose foods that by their colors and *yin/yang* balance fall somewhere in the middle range, we eliminate both stress and the tendency to be overemotional, and become happier and more in harmony. Perhaps it is no accident that the foods that do us most good are the greens and yellows of seeds, vegetables, nuts, pulses, cereals, beans, and fruit.

White foods, such as salt, eggs, fish, poultry, and hard cheeses, tend to be overly *yang*. Very dark foods, such as raw cane sugar, aromatic spices, and stimulants (e.g. coffee, tea, and cocoa), tend to be overly *yin*. However, by adding a *yang* white food, such as milk to a very dark, overly *yin* food, its excessive *yin* qualities can be reduced. Similarly, the very *yang* effect of foods such as meat, fish, and poultry is lessened if a *yin* food is added to them. This is one reason why it makes sense to serve apples with pork.

The color of food, according to Taoism, indicates whether it is yin or yang. The color-wheel above ranges from yang reds and oranges to yin blues and purples.

Very *yin* dark foods, such as raw cane sugar, become paler and more *yang* when they are processed or refined. Dark vinegar is very *yin*, but white vinegar is more *yang*, though of course it is still *yin* in essence. Alcoholic drinks are all *yin*, but the paler, usually grain-based, spirits have a better *yang* balance. The same is true of wines – the dark red wines are more *yin* while white wines have a better *yang* balance.

The Taste of Food

Taste also has its *yin* and *yang* aspects and is something else in which we should seek balance. Sweet foods tend to be *yin*, while strong-tasting foods, such as meats, are *yang*. The sweeter the fruit the more *yin* it is; the saltier the meat, the more *yang* it is. Obviously we don't want our diet to be bland and plain-tasting, and we need stimulation through all of our senses when we are eating, but the more strong-tasting the food the closer to one of the *yin* or *yang* extremes it veers. Occasional use of strong-tasting spices is fine; it only becomes a problem if someone is incapable of eating any food without heavily spicing it or uses pickles, chutneys, and sauces with everything.

Dark foods, such as raw cane sugar and cocoa, tend to be very yin, *whereas light foods, such as fish and dairy products, tend to be very* yang.

NO FORBIDDEN FOODS

In the Taoist approach there are no fierce dietary rules or forbidden foods – you can eat anything you want, cook with any spices you want, prepare any dish in any way you want. The Taoist approach is merely one of seeking balance and internal harmony. If you choose to eat foods that are excessively *yin* or *yang*, that's fine as long as you are aware of the possible detrimental effects they may have on your body, health, mental outlook, and emotional responses. Nothing is taboo; it is merely advised that restraint be observed, and if you feel that a particular food is used more than others, perhaps the reason for this could be examined.

It is quite interesting sometimes to observe what people eat. You might notice that people who are very *yang* in themselves often go for lots of stimulants like coffee and cigarettes, which are very *yin*, as well as relying on heavily spiced foods such as curries, which again are very *yin*. This is an attempt to generate internal coolness to alleviate some of their *yang* heat. This type of person may be suffering from stress or a similar condition which would lead to internal heat. Naturally, it is no good replacing a lack of *yin* with artificial stimulants – anyone suffering from such a deficiency should be encouraged to eat fresh produce that is a natural source of the *yin* element.

People who are predominantly *yin* in their aspect often go for a very *yang* diet to alleviate their internal cold, choosing cheese-based recipes or cooking a lot of poultry, or even using an excessive amount of salt in their cooking, to try to generate some internal warmth. As well as increasing the *yang* in their diet, this type of person might be advised to become more active in order to return to a good balance.

The Texture of Food

The texture of food is also important in the Taoist tradition. Food that is too soft or too hard veers toward a *yin* or *yang* extreme. We should eat food that needs chewing but doesn't hurt the teeth. Excessive amounts of food that is too soft and doesn't need any chewing at all should be avoided.

COOKING AS MEDITATION

Along with breathing and sleeping, eating is one of the most important activities carried out by human beings to keep themselves alive. The food we eat affects every aspect of our nature, from our health to our emotional responses. It makes sense to take care over how we prepare our food. You will find information later in this book about cooking equipment and general food preparation, but what about our mental and emotional approach? Cooking can be seen either as a chore or as a delightful experience that we enjoy and that is worth taking time and trouble over. Which is it to you?

Good Timing

If we think of cooking as something to be rushed through and done as quickly as possible to get it over with, then this sense of urgency and hurriedness will be conveyed to our food. We will feel the need to eat it all quickly and get away from the table as soon as possible. The Taoist approach is to take time and enjoy cooking so that the food is prepared in a relaxed and meditative way and arrives in an unhurried fashion. Then we can eat slowly, enjoy our digestion, linger over our meal, and focus on what good the food is doing us. It is no accident that people with the longest lifespans also tend to spend the longest over their meals, thoroughly enjoying each mouthful.

In warmer climates, such as the Mediterranean, people spend more time preparing their meals and at the same time they chat and enjoy their families much more. There simply isn't any sense of urgency; consequently their digestion is better and the rates of such diseases as bowel cancer much lower.

"When eating bamboo sprouts, remember the man that planted them"

The Taoist way is to make the preparation part of the eating process; natural ingredients should be prepared using natural tools such as wooden chopping boards and steel knives.

The Natural Cycle of Cooking

Cooking is a skill – some might say an art form – that is worth learning if only to improve the quality of our food. But cooking is also a means of learning about ourselves and being in touch with nature and our environment. If you are used to eating processed packaged food, it will at first seem odd to eat raw vegetables picked fresh from the garden. But it will not take long to adjust your palate to simpler, healthier dishes. You may also have to find time to cook new dishes in the proper Taoist way.

If we buy quick-to-prepare processed foods and heat them in a microwave we will feel divorced from a natural cycle of life that is extremely important to our well-being. If, on the other hand, we buy fresh produce and take time and care over its preparation, using natural, simple heating and cooking methods, we will feel connected and in touch, and we will be part of a long tradition that has served humanity for many thousands of years.

As you cook, be aware of that tradition; feel in touch with your ancestors who first learned about fire, first learned to cook, and spent time raising their families so you too could be here.

Eating outside, in harmony with nature, is an excellent way to maximize the energy available in food.

Respect Your Ingredients

As you chop vegetables, be aware of the life-giving *ch'i* they contain. View them as precious treasure houses of vital energy without which we simply couldn't live. Use them with respect and love. Be aware of how they grew and how they are being provided for you, to give you life. As you slice an apple in half, take time to wonder at its perfection and beauty, and be aware that you are the first human being ever to see inside it. Its life-giving energy has been provided by the universe especially for you alone to enjoy.

Chopping vegetables may seem a chore, but try to think of the life-giving energy that they emit during the task.

The Way of Preparation

The Taoist approach is that everything is as it should be. Make sure you have all the ingredients you need before you start, and allow yourself plenty of time to do the cooking with few interruptions — take the phone off the hook; you're about to do something important.

As you handle the food, be aware of its color, texture, and existence. This food is being prepared for you to eat and to give you life; it will become you, and whatever you eat will reflect the sort of person you are. Take time and use only the freshest ingredients of the highest quality you can afford. Take control of what you eat and don't be at the mercy of mega-business food producers who saturate food with preservatives and artificial color in order to improve their profits rather than your appetite, health, or emotional well-being.

Mindful Cooking

As you cook, breathe deeply and slowly. Work gently as if holding a newborn baby. Keep harsh noises to a minimum so that you feel tranquil and rested. Learn about *feng shui* (see page 18) so that your kitchen is harmonious and feels right.

Occasionally close your eyes and smell the fresh smells of good ingredients, sensing the life within them. Be at peace with your food, remembering where it has come from and why it is going to taste so good.

When you take this Taoist approach to cooking – taking time to wonder – the whole process becomes magical; an almost mystical experience of life itself.

Always try to prepare your vegetables in an uncluttered, tranquil space, on surfaces made from natural materials.

COOKING AND *KARMA*

The Taoists don't have quite the same notion of karma as the Buddhists do. To the Buddhists, *karma* is retribution for bad things done, to be worked off or repaid in subsequent lifetimes. To the Taoists, *karma* is an instant thing; if you do something wrong or bad you will suffer for it at once. This approach is most heavily present in the Taoist view of food: eat badly and you will feel unwell almost at once; eat well and you will feel instantly invigorated and recharged.

Energy Transformed

To the Buddhists, all life is sacred and they will not eat any animal products. This can cause their diet to be very heavily *yin*. (We will look at the Taoist approach to vegetarianism, and how it appertains to our dietary requirements, a little later; see page 42.) The Taoist approach to life is somewhat different. The Taoists believe that all life, all energy, is incapable of being destroyed – it can only be transformed from one type to another. The dying *yin* of an animal becomes the newborn *yang* of your food. Without this constant interchange of energy, the universe would stagnate.

A Time for Everything

Everything has to die, to be born, to live. The only consideration the Taoist has is the quality of that life. Deliberately providing an animal with a poor quality of life is regarded by the Taoists in the same way the Buddhists regard the taking of a life. If you cause suffering you will instantly be affected yourself, either in your emotional life or through ill health. If you live gently and cause no offense to others around you, then you will be happy and at peace with the universe. Taoists don't have a notion of a future heaven that exists as a reward for "being good." Instead they reason that being good is in our own best interests. This life can be all the heaven we need if we live it right. The Taoist approach is to live it right, right now.

Choosing your Tao

Animals that have enjoyed a good quality of life provide food that generates a good quality of energy.

The Taoists also say that you must choose your own path, your own way, your own Tao. It is pointless to adopt someone else's philosophy or religion. You have to make your own peace with the universe. This isn't to do with what you think may or may not be right, or with what you may or may not have been taught or told. You have to live a life that feels right to you.

"Gaze at the stars but walk on the earth"

Diet and *Karma*

When our diet is heavily dependent on overly *yin* or overly *yang* foods, it can affect our judgment. An overly *yin* diet will make us weak, emotionally dependent, and thus too ready to take on other people's attitudes and beliefs. A diet that is too *yang* will make us stubborn, set in our ways, and unable to be flexible and movable. A well-balanced diet will enable us to go with the flow, to steer our way gently through life without creating unnecessary offense or causing needless harm.

This is the Taoist way; to be and to enjoy without necessarily being part of the action; to be in the world but not of it; to take from the world whatever we need but no more; to try to put back a little if we can. These simple principles can be applied to all aspects of life from choosing where to live to and preparing a delicious meal.

The idea of a garden, as both a food source for the grower and a gift to the future, is central to Taoist philosophy.

Quality of Life

Karma means reaping not only the results of your actions but also the quality of your actions. If we lead hurried, wasteful lives, then the quality of our life is lost. By adopting a more Taoist approach and moving gently and slowly through our life we have time to appreciate it before it is all used up on pointless activities that bring no benefit.

The Taoists believe that what is, simply is. We cannot change the fundamental laws of the universe so we have to live and work with them. Energy moves and is in a state of constant change. Once we accept that, we can benefit from the interplay of that energy. We learn that seasons come and go and our moods and activities change with them.

If we plan to go out sunbathing and it's raining we can either get cross, which is pointless and of no benefit, or we can find something else to do indoors that is beneficial and useful. The Taoists say that in the summer we rise earlier and are more busy; in the winter we stay in bed longer and do less. This is natural and part of the perfect order of the universe. We aren't being lazy in the winter, nor are we being hyperactive in the summer. We are going with the flow.

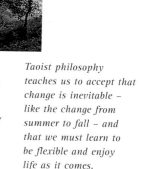

Taoist philosophy teaches us to accept that change is inevitable – like the change from summer to fall – and that we must learn to be flexible and enjoy life as it comes.

Instant *Karma*

The immediate effects of *karma* may become apparent if you try to cook hurriedly. If you rush your cooking, food gets burned or spoiled, fat gets splashed, and sometimes you get burned as well. If you prepare food in a distracted and disinterested way, the results will reflect your distraction and your food will be unsatisfactory. If you use poor ingredients that lack nutrition, your cooking will be equally as poor. Poor food leads to poor digestion – this is instant *karma*.

Karma and Digestion

If your digestion is poor the whole process of elimination will be upset and ill health will be the result. By using good ingredients, cooking well, and eating properly our digestion and elimination processes improve and our health becomes vital and good – instant *karma* again.

TAO, VEGETARIANISM, AND VEGANISM

Should we eat meat and other animal products? Is it right to do
so? Well, this is a book about the Taoist approach to cooking, and
the Taoists don't have rules about whether you should or should
not do something: it's for each of us to decide whether it is right
or not; whether it is something we wish to consider or not. If it
feels right, do it. If it feels wrong, then don't do it – that is the
Taoist approach.

According to Taoist beliefs, we should look at what sort of food
we eat and the way it affects our health. We saw earlier that
animal products, especially meat, are very *yang* in their quality.
If we eat a lot of meat, we too will become very *yang* and that
means we will generate a lot of internal heat. This can make us
aggressive, stubborn, and quite fixed in our mental attitude. An
extremely *yang* diet is not good for our digestive system; we
simply cannot process such a *yang*-enriched diet. *Yang* food
doesn't stay fresh for very long because the *yang ch'i* energy is
extremely volatile and ready to change to its *yin* opposite quickly.
If our diet is *yang*-enriched we need to process the food quickly
before the toxins build up in our system and poison us. Eating a
heavily enriched *yang* diet will cause our system to overload and
result in ill health because the food stays in our digestive system
too long and the resulting *yin* effects can be harmful.

However, the opposite is also true: a diet that is too *yin* will
also adversely affect our health. *Yin* food holds on to its qualities

longer than *yang* food; while *yang* is ever ready to change to *yin* – that's inherent in its nature – *yin*'s nature is not to change. If you eat only heavily *yin*-enriched foods you will find your system becomes extremely cold and this will cause ill health. You will also find yourself becoming more and more distant from reality. The nature of *yin* is space. The nature of *yang* is time. *Yin* food will encourage a remoteness from everyday life while *yang* food will cause a feeling of panic because there is so little time to do everything that you need to do.

As in all things, the Taoist approach is one of balance. We need to eat some *yang* food occasionally in the form of poultry, eggs, fish, hard cheese, and a little red meat, to stop our diet from becoming too *yin*. We also need the *yin* qualities of vegetables, grains, nuts, seeds, and beans to stop our diet from becoming too *yang*. If we rely on one type, *yin* or *yang*, we set up closed circles of behavior. Too much *yang* makes us stubborn so we cling to our ideas about diet and eat only meat. Too much *yin* makes us "spacy" so we continually seek foods that encourage fear and worry, which makes us more concerned about the fate of animals so we turn more and more to extreme *yin* diets such as vegetarianism and the more extreme veganism.

In Taoism there are no rules: you must do what you think and feel is right for you.

"Water is one essence but drunk by a cow it becomes milk, while drunk by a snake it becomes poison"

Yang *foods include fish, eggs, and pulses although these can also be yin. We need to eat yang food if we suffer from sluggishness and inertia. However, too much yang in our diet and we become stubborn and aggressive. Too much yin and we are anxious.*

THE
TAO
OF COOKING

*The Tao of cooking is about simplicity. The simpler
and closer to nature our diets are, then the happier we can
be. The more complex our diets and the further we are
removed from a natural life, then the more toxins and
stress we accumulate through food.*

THE TAO OF INGREDIENTS

Wouldn't it be refreshing to pop into the garden to collect the ingredients for supper rather than making the long trek in the car to the supermarket to buy canned and frozen produce that doesn't even taste like food anymore? Which would you choose?

There is simply nothing to beat growing your own ingredients in your own garden. You then have as much control as possible over their fertilizing and harvesting; you don't have to eat vegetables laced with preservatives, coloring, or chemicals such as phosphates. In an ideal world that's what we would all do: grow vegetables; keep a couple of chickens for their eggs; train some fruit bushes against the garden fence; plant an apple tree or two; go fishing in the local stream; collect nuts in the fall from the woods; grow herbs in pots on the kitchen windowsill; have a hive for honey; even keep a cow for the milk. That's the Taoist way: simple, efficient, kindly, soothing, and a way of life that doesn't interfere with or threaten the rest of the world.

Fresh, Organic, and Good

Ingredients should be as fresh, as organic, and as vitamin-packed as possible. If you can't buy organic at least try to buy fresh. If you can't get fresh try to buy good quality. And if you can't get good quality, change where you shop. The ingredients are the raw materials of the meals you are going to eat to give you the energy for your life. You wouldn't put water in the fuel tank of your car and expect it to run properly, and yet we eat poor-quality foods and expect our bodies to perform just as well.

The closer to their natural state raw ingredients are, the better they are and the more vital their ch'i. They should smell of the earth and taste of the sun; leafy vegetables should be still wet with dew; fruit should be picked from the tree and eaten in its shade.

The Seasons

Ingredients should be bought fresh and in season. That's what the seasons are for – to provide variety. If we eat strawberries all year round there is no excitement and no anticipation when the first ones arrive in the early summer. If we can eat frozen food whenever we want, we lose our zest and enthusiasm for fresh food as well as losing our sense of the passing of the seasons. If we shop only in supermarkets we forget about nature – harvests and the smell of fresh picked grain rubbed in the palm of your hand.

COOKING METHODS AND EQUIPMENT

The more complex our lives, the greater the effects of stress; the simpler our lives and the closer we are to a natural existence, the less stress we incur and thus the happier we are. The same goes for our cooking equipment.

Yin and *Yang* Fire

We need heat to cook and there are a variety of ways to generate it, ranging from a simple open wood fire to a complex electric oven. Heat is a very *yang* aspect, and the more modern the heating source the more *yang* it is. A wood fire is also *yang* but well-balanced toward being *yin*. Ideally, the more flame we can see the better, since it is more *yin*, more balanced. The more removed from flames the heat source is, the more *yang* it is, which is why microwaves are unsatisfactory from the Taoist viewpoint. A gas stove might be used in preference to an electric one because of this, but many people have electric stoves in their homes and might be obliged to use them. However, they should bear in mind that electric stoves are quite *yang* and will have a very drying effect on food, especially anything that is slow-roasted.

The same is also true of cooking methods. Deep-frying is obviously much more *yang* than leaving the food raw, which is very *yin*. Baking and pressure-cooking are also *yang*, whereas boiling is quite a *yin* way to cook. Stir-frying and steaming are extremely well-balanced.

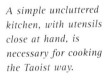

A simple uncluttered kitchen, with utensils close at hand, is necessary for cooking the Taoist way.

STEEL STEAMER

STIR-FRY PAN

WOODEN STEAMER

LARGE IRON WOK

Pots and Pans

Pots and pans should be chosen for their simplicity and efficiency and should be made from natural materials, such as wood and iron.

Again, the closer to nature your pots and pans are, the better. Simple earthenware pots and iron pans are best. The more complex the pots and pans, such as those with nonstick surfaces, the further removed they are from simplicity and consequently the less Taoist they are in approach.

Stirring implements should ideally be made of wood. If you are able to do so, avoid using any plastic-coated cooking utensils. Wooden plates and bowls are best, but earthenware or chinaware is fine if you prefer. Plastic cups, plates, and bowls are not really considered part of the Taoist tradition, besides which, we simply do not know the long-term effect of eating our food off such unnatural materials.

Large, open pans for quick stir-frying are very good because they allow the food to be stirred thoroughly and evenly and the heat to spread quickly throughout the food.

If you're faced with a choice when it comes to buying pots and pans, remember the symbol of the peach and ask yourself how far removed from the tree is whatever you want to buy. If it is far removed and made by a complex manufacturing process, it is probably not in your best interest to use it. If, however, it is simply made and uses natural materials and feels right, then it probably is right. Simple is best; natural is fine.

"Immersed in water, you stretch out your hands for a drink"

FOOD PREPARATION

There are a few guidelines for food preparation that, although based on common sense and established theories of food hygiene, fit into the Taoist approach.

Natural Materials

Modern kitchens are designed to look shiny and pristine, but this often means that they are filled with synthetic materials. Try to use natural materials, such as marble work surfaces and wooden chopping boards, to do all your food preparation on; these are simple, natural, and easy to clean.

Simple and Fresh

If food comes into contact with complex plastics there is always a risk of a residue from the material being conveyed to our food. This isn't ideal. Most people like to keep their food cold in a refrigerator, which, in effect, is putting it into a very large metal and plastic box.

The reason we need such large storage containers is that we are far too busy to shop frequently and need to keep the food cold to prevent it from spoiling. A much more natural way is to buy the food you are going to eat on the day you are going to eat it – buy it fresh and eat it that way (or, better still, harvest it fresh from the garden). This way you can free yourself from the need for a refrigerator or freezer.

Don't keep food and reheat it the next day. Give it to the chickens or dog and buy yourself something fresh.

Separating *Yin* from *Yang*

Keep cooked meats and raw meats separate; ideally, don't have or use them at the same time. Keep meats away from vegetables – don't mix your *yin* and *yang*. If you choose to keep meats in the refrigerator, keep them on a lower shelf than any vegetables – *yang* below *yin* for storage.

Whatever chopping equipment you use for meat, have a separate selection for vegetables – that means separate knives and chopping boards.

Have a separate sink in your kitchen for washing hands – don't wash them in the same sink that you use to wash vegetables. Wash your hands between handling meat and vegetables. Wash all equipment as you use it rather than leaving it for later.

A clean, uncluttered kitchen means you can prepare and cook food in a relaxed manner, and the resulting dishes will be replete with vital energy.

Take Time to be Clear

Food preparation is as much a part of cooking as the actual boiling, frying, and baking. Take your time over chopping vegetables so that you enjoy the experience. You can't do this if you are cramped for space or working in clutter.

Before you settle down to preparing your meal, clear your work surfaces of everything except the items that you actually need at that very moment. Remember: the clearer the space you have to work in, the clearer your mind when you are cooking. And having a clear mind is very important; the clearer your mind the clearer the food. If you are rushed, bad-tempered, and stressed when you are cooking, it will be conveyed to the food. Be clear, be uncluttered, and be relaxed.

Ch'i energy can be encouraged or discouraged from flowing into your home by what you have in your kitchen. If your kitchen is dark and messy, the *ch'i* will not feel welcome and your kitchen energy will be stagnant. If your kitchen is light, uncluttered, and fresh, the *ch'i* will feel at home and will fill your kitchen with invigorating energy.

CABBAGE

RED PEPPER

CUCUMBER

TOMATOES

OLIVES

Give food ingredients a chance to show their individual color and beauty by arranging them on a pale, plain background and leaving space around each one.

PRESENTATION AND SERVING

Food is not just for eating. It is also a visual feast that should look as good as it tastes. Colors should be fresh and vibrant, and there should be lots of clear space around the food so that you can see it clearly. An overfilled plate is not only bad for you in the sense of overeating, but it also overloads you visually.

Plain Plates
Simple white or plain, light-colored wooden plates are best because they allow the food to proclaim its own glory without it having to be adorned with accessories. Each item of food on a plate should be seen in its entirety and not smothered by other items. Leave lots of space around the edges of the plate to give the food a chance to "breathe."

Everything you are going to need to eat should be on the table when you start. There is nothing worse than the cook constantly getting up to bring in items that have been forgotten. It also allows your guests to see exactly what they have to eat in its entirety and thus judge the size of portions they want and how much to eat of any one course.

Simple Courses
It is better to have lots of small courses with each food being seen and eaten on its own than to pile up plates with everything at once. This only puts people off or encourages overeating.

陽

"Find the silence that contains thoughts"

Simple courses also encourage conversation, which is an essential ingredient of any meal. You want your guests to feel relaxed and to enjoy themselves. If you give them a full trough they will behave like pigs; if you give them delicate, subtle, simple courses they will behave in a refined way and you will get lots of stimulating conversation.

Ideally, food should be served in an atmosphere of great calm and reverence. Each course should be presented with a few brief words to describe it but don't explain it exhaustively – let the food speak for itself.

Allow time between courses for your guests to express their enjoyment of the food and to let the food settle before the next course. Be in the now – never mind the last course or the next. Don't cook meals that entail eating one course while you are finishing the cooking of the next.

Simple Tables

When you serve food it should be on a table that is set aside for eating. If your children also happen to use it to do their homework, then that should be cleared away before you eat. There shouldn't be anything on the table that isn't relevant to the meal. A clear, fresh table looks best when it has space and isn't cluttered. Don't make the mistake of thinking you have to fill up all the surface area with baskets of bread or pots of flowers. Leave it clear and let it speak for itself.

Keep your tableware light and plain so that the food served on it can be fully appreciated. Even if you are having a dinner party and want to impress your guests, try to keep the dining table as simple as possible.

THE TAO OF EATING

You might think that eating is just something we do. Surely there are no rules or guidelines? Well, actually there are some ideas to think about if you want your eating, and thus your digestion, to improve and life to be more comfortable.

Take your Time

Eating is a pleasurable activity – or at least it should be. The food should be savored, tasted, enjoyed, relished, smelled, and delighted in. You should have a relationship with your food – after all it is about to become a part of you, to give you life and energy. If you rush the eating, you cannot enjoy it. Eat slowly. Chew well. Taste each mouthful. This approach also leads to better digestion of your food.

   If you linger over your food and take time to enjoy it, you want it to be of the highest standard. If you are prepared to settle for second-rate convenience food, then you might as well eat it quickly before you have time to taste it and realize what harm it is doing and how bland it is.

Prepare to Eat

Before you eat you might like to just close your eyes for a second and breathe deeply; prepare your stomach emotionally for what is to come; relax your whole system to receive the new energy; still your mind so you can concentrate on what you are about to do and then you can be focused on your food.

Enjoy!

When a plate of food is first put in front of you, take time to enjoy the look of it. Spend a moment or two just savoring the colors and textures; luxuriate in the knowledge that it is going to provide you with lots of energy. Take a minute to check that you really are hungry and not just eating out of habit. Check that the food before you has the right balance of *yin* and *yang* and that it is seasonally right for you.

Chopping Wood, Eating Rice

Eat when you are hungry. Sleep when you are tired. These are Taoist suggestions and they make sense. Don't overeat. Don't starve yourself. Food is there for you to enjoy, to give you life and energy, and to stimulate your palate and taste buds. Food should be interesting and wholesome, nourishing and fresh. If it isn't, why are you eating it? Food should be cooked in an atmosphere of calm and love. If not, why isn't it? Food should be eaten slowly and thoughtfully, with relish and respect. If you rush it, why? If you aren't hungry go and chop wood for the fire. The Taoist precept is: before enlightenment – chopping wood and eating rice; after enlightenment – chopping wood and eating rice.

RECIPES

For each of the following recipes, approximate cooking times have been given. We are, however, adopting a Taoist approach, and urge you to do likewise – when the food is cooked, it is cooked. If you expect something to take exactly 20 minutes to cook and it still isn't ready after 24 minutes, it simply doesn't matter. When cooking in the Taoist manner, you learn to feel when the food is ready. In the same way, if a recipe calls for four tomatoes and you only have three, that's fine – use the three you have.

All recipes serve four people unless otherwise stated.

BASIC RECIPES

Bouquet Garni

No cook would be without their bouquet garni, that little bag of herbs and spices used to flavor warming winter casseroles and stews.

1 bay leaf
sprig of thyme
6 peppercorns

1. Place the ingredients in a bag made from a small square of cheesecloth (muslin), or a leek leaf, and tie up with string.
2. Hang inside the pan tied to the handle while cooking so the bouquet garni can be retrieved prior to serving.

Chicken Stock

Makes about
5 cups/
2 pints
(1.1 liters)
Ⓙ **Cooking time:**
2–3 hours

1 roast chicken carcass with all trimmings and bones
1 onion, peeled and sliced
1 carrot, peeled and sliced
1 stalk celery, sliced
1 bouquet garni
1 bay leaf
salt and pepper to taste

1. Cut the chicken into large pieces and put in a large saucepan with all the trimmings and bones. Add 3 pints (1.7 liters) water and the onion, carrot, celery, bouquet garni, bay leaf, and a little salt and pepper.
2. Bring to a boil and skim the surface to remove froth. Reduce the heat, partially cover, and simmer for 2–3 hours. Strain and leave to cool.
3. When cold, remove all traces of fat from the surface of the stock.

Vegetable Stock

Makes about
5 cups/
Ⓙ 2 pints
(1.1 liters)
Cooking time:
1½–2 hours

2 tbsp (30 ml) vegetable oil
1 onion, peeled and finely chopped
1 carrot, peeled and chopped
½ cup/2 oz (50 g) peeled and diced turnip
½ cup/2 oz (50 g) peeled and diced parsnip
4 stalks celery, chopped
1 bouquet garni
6 black peppercorns
a little salt

1. Heat the oil in a saucepan, add the onion, and fry gently for about 5 minutes or until the onion is lightly browned.
2. Add all the other ingredients and 3 pints (1.7 liters) water.
3. Bring to a boil, then reduce the heat, partially cover and simmer for about 1½ hours, skimming occasionally. Strain and leave to cool.
4. Cover and keep in the refrigerator. Use within 48 hours.

陽

"Whoever talks of right and wrong doesn't understand the Tao"

THE TAO OF SOUPS

Soups are marvelous food and they have a unique role to play in Taoist cooking because they are capable of being either *yin* or *yang* and can even be both at the same time. You can have warm *yang* soups in the winter and cooling *yin* soups in the summer.

Fresh Ingredients

Canned and ready-made soups aren't really soups at all. Soups should always be made from the freshest ingredients you can find; soups weren't designed to be made with leftover scraps. If a soup is worth making, it is worth making with fresh ingredients, rather than something left over from a previous meal.

Yin and Yang Soups

Soup can be a lovely thick broth – more stew than soup – but still a warming *yang* dish for a cold winter's day. You can use meat in soups to produce some delicious and very *yang* recipes, and keep the vegetables for the cool, clear summer soups.

Keep it Simple

Soups are probably best when they are kept simple. Chicken soup is a good example of this. If you add lots of other ingredients it ceases to be chicken soup and becomes a casserole. Chicken soup made almost clear and with a tiny film of fat on the top is a wonderful pick-me-up for invalids and sick children. For anyone who is sick it might be the only food they can manage.

Eat Medicine

Chinese herbalists recommend soups for nearly all conditions because they make taking herbs much more palatable.

Herbalists call their soups "medicine;" what better way could there be to take medicine than in a bowl of delicious soup?

Making and Serving Soup

It's not just the eating of soups that is important; without doubt, guests really appreciate the time you take over soup-making. Light soups can be served as starters, to whet the appetite, while heavier soups can be meals in themselves. If you serve soup from a tureen, use soup bowls with wide edges so everyone has room for crusty bread on the side. You could add *yang* meatballs, garlic, cheese, or croûtons to your soups to counteract winter chills.

Always use the freshest ingredients in your soups; this way you benefit from delicious soups that are really good for you.

Orange and Cucumber Soup

This is a very yin recipe combining refreshing citrus and summer vegetable flavors; ideal for a hot day.

Season:
Summer

Preparation time:
10–20 minutes plus chilling

⅔ cucumber
4 oranges
salt
2 lemons
1¼ cups/½ pint (300 ml) cold peppermint tea

1. Peel and thinly slice the cucumber and two of the oranges.
2. Spread the cucumber slices on a flat plate, sprinkle them with salt, and place another heavy plate on top.
3. Squeeze the juice from the lemons and the remaining two oranges, and mix with the cold peppermint tea.
4. Rinse the cucumber thoroughly, then add the cucumber and orange slices to the liquid.
5. Chill in the refrigerator before serving.

Avocado Soup

This soup can be served hot or chilled.

Season:
Summer

Preparation time:
10–20 minutes

large ripe avocados
4¼ cups/1¾ pints (1 liter) chicken stock (see page 55)
1 cup/8 fl oz (250 ml) half-and-half (single cream)
salt and pepper to taste
1 tbsp (15 ml) finely chopped cilantro (coriander) to serve

1. Halve and pit the avocados, and mash the flesh inside the skin. Press the flesh through a strainer into a large bowl, and then discard the skins.
2. Put the chicken stock and half-and-half into a saucepan, and heat gently, without boiling.
3. Pour the stock and half-and-half (single cream) onto the avocado, beating thoroughly.
4. Add salt and pepper to taste, and serve sprinkled with cilantro (coriander).

Carrot and Celeriac Soup

This is a wonderfully yin *soup that can be served cool in the summer.*

Season:
Summer

Cooking time:
50-60
minutes

2 tbsp (30 ml) vegetable oil

2 cups/½ lb (225 g) peeled and chopped onions

2 lb (900 g) peeled and chopped carrots

2 lb (900 g) celeriac, peeled and chopped

3 pints (1.7 liters) chicken stock (see page 55)

grated zest and juice of 1 medium orange

1¼ cups/½ pint (300 ml) half-and-half (single cream)

salt and pepper to taste

1. Heat the oil in a large saucepan, and add the vegetables. Sauté for about 5 minutes.

2. Add the chicken stock and bring to a boil, then reduce the heat, cover and simmer gently for about 25 minutes.

3. Add the orange zest and juice, and simmer for a further 20 minutes or so.

4. Remove from the heat and leave to cool slightly, then purée the mixture in a blender until smooth.

5. Let cool completely, then add the half-and-half (single cream), and salt and pepper to taste.

Chicken and Coconut Soup

A marvelously warming yang *soup. The coconut gives it a delicious creaminess.*

Season:
Winter

Cooking time:
30–40 minutes

3 cups/1½ pints (750 ml) coconut milk

2 cups/16 fl oz (475 ml) chicken stock (see page 55)

4 stalks lemon grass, bruised

1 inch (2.5 cm) piece of galangal, peeled and thinly sliced

10 black peppercorns, crushed

10 kaffir lime leaves

11 oz (300 g) chicken, skinned, boned, and cut into thin strips

¼ lb (100 g) button mushrooms

½ cup/2 oz (50 g) baby sweetcorn

¼ cup/4 tbsp (60 ml) lime juice

GARNISH

2 red chilies, seeded and chopped

chopped green (spring) onions

chopped cilantro (coriander) leaves

1. Put the coconut milk and chicken stock into a large saucepan and bring to a boil.
2. Add the lemon grass, galangal, peppercorns, and half the kaffir lime leaves. Reduce the heat and simmer for around 15 minutes.
3. Strain the broth, then return it to the heat and add the chicken, mushrooms, and corn. Cook for 10 minutes or until the chicken is cooked.
4. Stir in the lime juice and the rest of the lime leaves. Serve hot, garnished with chopped chili, green (spring) onion, and cilantro (coriander).

Chilled Almond Soup

A very yin, *cooling soup for a hot day. Although it takes a few minutes to prepare, remember to allow some time for it to cool.*

Season:
Summer

Preparation time:
10–20 minutes

¾ cup/¼ lb (100 g) blanched almonds

4 cloves garlic, peeled

1 tbsp (15 ml) olive oil

1 tbsp (15 ml) white wine vinegar

2 slices white bread, broken into pieces

3 cups/1½ pints (750 ml) chicken stock (see page 55)

salt and pepper to taste

GARNISH

1 tbsp (15 ml) chopped parsley

¾ lb (350 g) seedless white grapes

1. Put the almonds, garlic, oil, and vinegar into a blender and process until smooth.

2. Add the bread and stock, a little at a time, blending again between each addition, until smooth. Add salt and pepper to taste.

3. Pour into individual serving bowls and garnish with parsley and grapes.

Salsify Lemon Soup

A very yin *soup to be served before a heavy* yang *meat meal. It has the added advantage of clearing your palate before the main course.*

Season:
Winter

Cooking time:
50–60 minutes

5 cups/2 pints (1.1 liters) chicken stock (see page 55)

¼ cup/3 tbsp (45 ml) lemon juice

1½ lb (750 g) salsify

2 tbsp (30 ml) chopped celery leaves

1 onion, peeled and chopped

1 tsp (5 ml) paprika

salt and pepper to taste

½ bunch watercress, finely chopped

⅔ cup/¼ pint (150 ml) half-and-half (single cream)

1. Put the stock and lemon juice into a large saucepan. Peel and roughly chop the salsify and add to the pan with the celery leaves, onion, and paprika. Add salt and pepper to taste and bring to a boil. Reduce the heat, cover and simmer for 45 minutes or until the salsify is tender. Remove from the heat and let cool slightly.

2. Purée the soup into a blender and return to the saucepan. Add the watercress and half-and-half (single cream), and simmer for another 5 minutes or so. Serve hot.

陽

"Forget injuries, never forget kindness"

Spicy Chicken Soup

A well-balanced yin/yang *soup which can be served on its own or as a starter before a* yang *meat dish.*

Season:
Winter

Preparation time:
30–40 minutes

1 tbsp (15 ml) vegetable oil

1 green chili, seeded and finely chopped

1 inch (2.5 cm) piece of fresh gingerroot, peeled and finely chopped

¾ lb (350 g) chicken breast, skinned, boned, and cut into small pieces

2 cloves garlic, peeled and crushed

3 cups/1½ pints (750 ml) chicken stock (see page 55)

¼ cup/3 tbsp (45 ml) lime juice

½ cup/6 tbsp (90 ml) chopped fresh cilantro (coriander)

½ lb (225 g) sliced snow peas (mangetout)

salt and pepper to taste

chopped green onions, to garnish

1. Heat the oil in a large saucepan and add the chili, ginger, chicken, and garlic. Cook for 5 minutes, or until the chicken is cooked.

2. Add the chicken stock, lime juice, and half the cilantro (coriander), and bring to a boil. Then reduce the heat, cover and simmer for 15 minutes or so.

3. Add the snow peas (mangetout) and cook for about another 5 minutes.

4. Add the remaining cilantro (coriander), and add salt and pepper to taste.

5. Serve hot, sprinkled with a garnish of chopped green onions.

Asparagus and Almond Soup

This is a warming yin *soup, ideal for a cold fall day. As well as being a delicacy, asparagus is a traditional folk medicine.*

Season:
Fall

Cooking time:
30–40 minutes

¾ cup/¼ lb (100 g) blanched almonds

5 cups/2 pints (1.1 liters) vegetable stock (see page 55)

1 tbsp (15 ml) vegetable oil

4 celery stalks chopped

1 lb (450 g) asparagus, trimmed and chopped

2 tbsp (30 ml) chopped fresh parsley

¼ cup/3 tbsp (45 ml) half-and-half (single cream)

salt and pepper to taste

GARNISH

cream

toasted flaked almonds

chopped parsley

1. Put the almonds and stock into a blender and purée until smooth. Strain, keeping the stock to use later.

2. Heat the oil in a large saucepan, add the celery, and fry for around 5 minutes.

3. Add the asparagus and cook for a further 5 minutes or so.

4. Pour in the stock and add the parsley. Cover and simmer for around 15 minutes. Remove from the heat and let cool slightly.

5. Purée in a blender until smooth, then return to gentle heat, and add the half-and-half (single cream) and salt and pepper to taste.

6. Serve hot, garnished with cream, toasted almonds, and parsley.

Sorrel, Potato, Rice, and Lettuce Soup

This very filling soup can be served cool in the summer garnished with Parmesan cheese.

Season:
Summer

Cooking time:
25–35
minutes

⅓ cup/4 tbsp (60 ml) vegetable oil

6 green (spring) onions, chopped

1 clove garlic, peeled and crushed

1 tsp (5 ml) chopped fresh thyme

¼ cup/2 oz (50 g) long grain rice

2 cups/½ lb (225 g) peeled and finely chopped potatoes

1 lb (450 g) coz lettuce, shredded

shredded sorrel

5 cups/2 pints (1.1 liters) vegetable stock (see page 55)

2 tbsp (30 ml) chopped fresh chives

pinch of grated nutmeg

salt and pepper to taste

freshly grated Parmesan cheese, to garnish

1. Heat the oil in a large saucepan, add the green onions, garlic, and thyme, and fry gently for 5 minutes, or until soft but not too brown.

2. Add the rice and potatoes, and stir-fry for about 2 minutes.

3. Stir in the lettuce and sorrel and add the stock. Bring to a boil, then reduce the heat, cover and simmer gently for 15 minutes, or until the rice and potatoes are cooked. Remove from the heat and leave to cool slightly.

4. Purée the soup in a blender with the chives, nutmeg, and salt and pepper to taste, until smooth. Leave to cool completely.

5. Serve garnished with Parmesan cheese and accompanied by hot French bread.

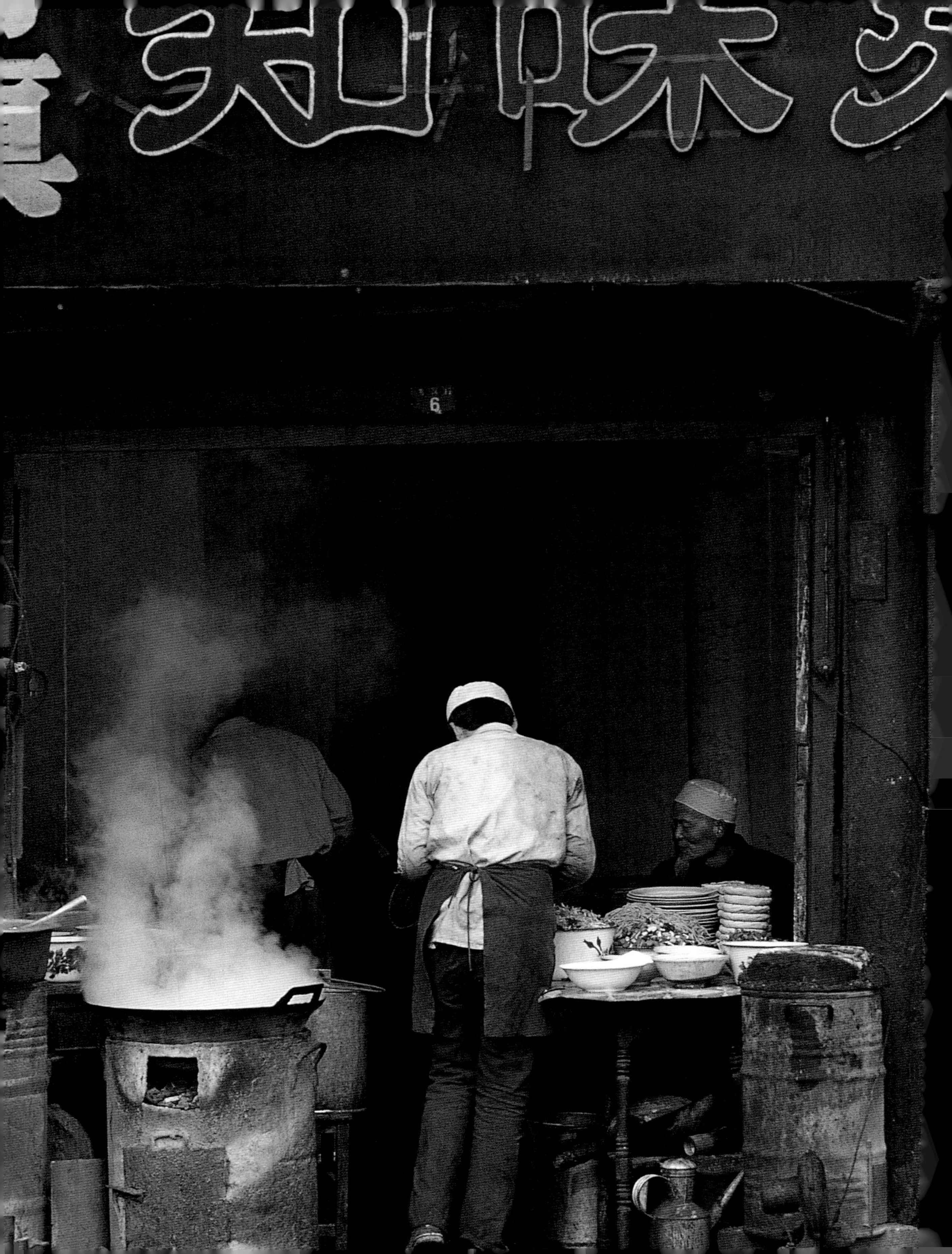

THE TAO OF MEAT AND POULTRY

Meat is fundamental to Taoist cooking. It provides a *yang* aspect to food and is a very important source of the protein we need.

If possible, all the meat and poultry you buy should be of the highest quality, preferably organic if you can get it. If you can buy meat that has come from animals which haven't been intensively farmed, so much the better. Animals kept in their natural habitat produce better meat.

Any meat which has been salted will have had its *yang* qualities increased and should be avoided. Meat should be a fresh item and eaten as soon as possible after being provided. Meat from internal organs is considered more *yin*, while meat from the muscles and surface areas is considered more *yang*.

Cooking Meat

When meat is roasted it loses a lot of its energy so it is often better to stir-fry it quickly. Cut the meat into small pieces and add it to hot oil, turning it once or twice. This type of cooking is known as "searing" and it preserves both the energy and the flavor of the meat. Roasting also has a very drying quality which affects the energy of the meat. Meat should be juicy, so if you are going to roast make sure the meat stays moist. Frozen meat is best avoided as the energy has been killed.

The more fat meat has, the greater its *yin* qualities, although, because it is an animal product, all meat is quite heavily *yang*. The leaner, darker, richer, and redder the meat, the more *yang* it is. If you don't want a diet that is too heavily *yang*, go for paler, whiter meats, choosing cuts that are not too lean.

Poultry

All types of poultry can be included in your diet, bearing in mind that the redder the meat the more *yang* it is. Chicken is more *yin* than duck and, although goose has a very dark flesh, it is quite *yin* because of its fat content.

Poultry, like any meat, should be as fresh as possible and from birds which have led a natural a life. Meat shouldn't be eaten too often as the *yang* qualities are very concentrated. Once or twice a week is sufficient.

Meat provides the important yang *element of the diet, but should be eaten in moderation.*

Pork and Bacon Sausages

Sausages barbecued then eaten outdoors — an ideal way to spend a warm summer evening. Serve with a dip.

Season:
Summer/
Fall

Cooking time:
30–40
minutes

⅔ cup/¼ lb (100 g) finely chopped rindless smoked fatty bacon

1 lb (450 g) lean ground pork

½ lb (225 g) pork sausage

1 small red chili, seeded and chopped

2 cloves garlic, peeled and crushed

½ cup/1 oz (25 g) fresh white bread crumbs

salt and pepper to taste

2 eggs, beaten

1. Mix together the bacon, ground pork, sausage, chili, garlic, and bread crumbs. Add salt and pepper to taste, and beat in the eggs.

2. Shape the mixture into about 20 sausages. Cover and leave for about 15 minutes to firm up.

3. Cook over hot coals or under the broiler for about 10 minutes or until thoroughly cooked, turning frequently.

Pork Chops with Plums

A very savory, but not too heavy, fall dish that includes spicy ginger to keep the cold out.

Season:
Summer/
Fall

Cooking time:
1-1¼ hours

1 lb (450 g) plums

1 inch (2.5 cm) piece of fresh gingerroot, peeled and shredded

1 tbsp (15 ml) vegetable oil

salt and pepper to taste

1 tbsp/½ oz (15 g) butter

4 pork chops, about 7 oz (200 g) each

⅓ cup/4 tbsp (60 ml) white wine

¾ cup/6 fl oz (175 ml) vegetable stock (see page 55)

2 tbsp (30 ml) Greek yogurt

2 tbsp (30 ml) chopped tarragon

1. Preheat the oven to 400°F, 200°C, gas mark 6.

2. Halve and pit the plums, and cut into slices. Mix with the ginger and spread in the bottom of a lightly oiled ovenproof dish. Add salt and pepper to taste.

3. Bake in the oven for about 15 minutes.

4. Meanwhile, heat the butter and the remaining oil in a skillet and add the pork chops. Brown on both sides, then place the pork chops on top of the cooked plums.

5. Add the white wine to the skillet and cook briskly until the liquid has reduced by half. Add the stock and cook for about 2 minutes, then pour the sauce over the pork chops.

6. Return to the oven for a further 30 minutes or until the pork is tender.

7. Serve hot on individual plates with a spoonful of yogurt and a little tarragon on each chop.

陽

> "How beautiful it is to do nothing, and then rest afterwards"

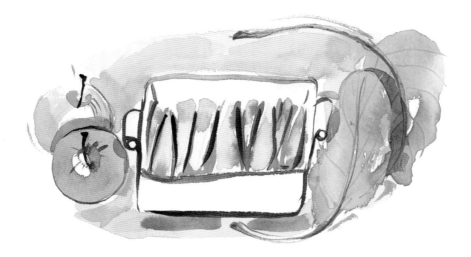

Pork and Parsnip Bake

This warming winter casserole dish includes apples to balance the yang meat.

Season:
Winter

Cooking time:
55-65
minutes

2 tbsp (30 ml) olive oil

4 lean pork chops

1 lb (450 g) parsnips, peeled and thinly sliced

salt and pepper to taste

½ lb (225 g) spinach, roughly chopped

2 medium cooking apples, peeled, cored, and sliced

1. Preheat the oven to 360°F, 180°C, gas mark 4.

2. Heat the oil in a skillet and fry the pork chops gently until brown on both sides. Remove the chops from the pan, saving the oil in the pan.

3. Brush a little of the oil over the bottom of a casserole dish, and arrange about half the parsnips in the bottom. Sprinkle the parsnips with salt and pepper to taste and place the chops on top.

4. Mix the spinach with the apples and place on top of the chops, adding a little more salt and pepper. Top with the remaining parsnips, and cover. Bake in the oven around for 30 minutes.

5. Take the lid off the casserole and brush the leftover oil from the frying pan over the parsnips. Return to the oven, uncovered, for about 15 minutes to brown before serving.

Liver with Orange

This dish can help invalids and convalescents restore their energy by raising their yang *levels.*

Season:
Summer

Cooking time:
15–25 minutes

4 tbsp/1 oz (25 g) plain flour
salt and pepper to taste
2 tsp (10 ml) chopped sage
1 lb (450 g) lamb's liver, thinly sliced
1 tbsp (15 ml) vegetable oil
2 cups/½ lb (225 g) peeled and chopped onions
grated zest and juice of 2 large oranges
GARNISH
orange slices
chopped fresh sage

1. Season the flour with a little salt and pepper, add the sage, and mix thoroughly. Toss the liver in the seasoned flour.
2. Heat the oil in a heavy skillet and add the onion. Cook for 3–4 minutes or until the onion is browned.
3. Add the liver and cook over a high heat for 5–6 minutes, stirring all the time, until the liver is lightly cooked.
4. Reduce the heat and stir in the orange zest and juice. Heat through but don't allow the orange to cook.
5. Serve hot, garnished with orange slices and a little fresh sage.

Minted Lamb with Yogurt

A delicious main course for the summer – filling but not too heavy. Serve with a tomato and onion salad.

Season:
Summer

Cooking time:
10–15 minutes plus marinating

1 lb (450 g) lamb escalopes, very thinly sliced
½ cup/6 tbsp (90 ml) natural Greek yogurt
1 clove garlic, peeled and crushed
¼ cup/4 tbsp (60 ml) chopped fresh mint
2 tbsp (30 ml) lemon juice
salt and pepper to taste

1. Mix the lamb with the yogurt, garlic, mint, lemon juice, and salt and pepper to taste. Cover and leave in the refrigerator to marinate for 2–3 hours.
2. Grill or broil the lamb for 3–4 minutes on each side until cooked and brown. Serve hot.

Beef Broth

A very warming yang *stew for a chilly fall day after a hard session in the garden.*

Season:
Fall

Cooking time:
2¼–2½ hours

4 tbsp/1 oz (25 g) plain flour

salt and pepper to taste

1 lb (450 g) braising steak, cubed

1 tbsp (15 ml) vegetable oil

3 cups/¾ lb (350 g) peeled and chopped carrots

1¼ lb (550 g) rutabaga (swede), peeled and chopped

4 stalks celery, chopped

½ lb (225 g) small onions, peeled

1 clove garlic, peeled and crushed

2½ cups/1 pint (600 ml) vegetable stock (see page 55)

grated zest and juice of 1 orange

⅔ cup/¼ pint (150 ml) red wine

2 large sprigs of rosemary

rosemary, to garnish

1. Preheat the oven to 325°F, 170°C, gas mark 3.

2. Season the flour with salt and pepper. Toss the beef in the seasoned flour until coated.

3. Heat the oil in a large flameproof casserole dish, add the beef and cook, stirring, until it turns brown. Remove the beef from the pan and drain.

4. Add the carrots, rutabaga (swede), celery, onions, and garlic to the casserole dish, and sauté the mixture for about 5 minutes.

5. Return the beef to the casserole dish with the vegetable stock, orange zest and juice, wine, and rosemary. Bring to a boil, then cover and cook in the oven for about 2 hours or until the beef is cooked through and tender.

6. Serve garnished with rosemary.

Chicken and Zucchini Stir-fry

Use fresh, organic, free-range chicken in this light recipe. Rice provides a good balance of yin *and* yang.

Season:
Spring

Cooking time:
10–20
minutes

1 tsp (5 ml) vegetable oil

1 clove garlic, peeled and finely chopped

1½ lb (750 g) zucchini (courgettes), cut into batons

1 lb (450 g) cooked chicken, cut into strips

¼ cup/3 tbsp (45 ml) half-and-half (single cream)

salt and pepper to taste

1. Heat the oil in a skillet small frying pan and add the garlic. Cook for a few seconds, then add the zucchini (courgettes) and cook for about 2 minutes.
2. Add the chicken and heat through, then reduce the heat and add the half-and-half (single cream) and salt and pepper to taste.

Chicken and Apple Casserole

A wonderful fall dish that is warming and nourishing.

Season:
Fall

Cooking time:
1¼–1½ hours

2 tbsp (30 ml) olive oil

4 chicken portions, about ½ lb (225 g) each

2 lb (900 g) seasonal root vegetables, e.g. parsnips, turnips, rutabaga (swede), peeled and diced

3 cups/¾ lb (350 g) peeled and chopped onions

⅔ cup/¼ lb (100 g) green lentils

2 small eating apples, peeled, cored, and sliced

scant cup apple juice

1¼ cups/½ pint (300 ml) chicken stock (see page 55)

salt and pepper to taste

1. Preheat the oven to 375°F, 190°C, gas mark 5.
2. Heat the oil in a large flameproof casserole and add the chicken pieces. Brown well, then remove and drain.
3. Add the root vegetables and onions to the casserole and sauté for around 5 minutes.
4. Add the lentils, apples, apple juice, and chicken stock, and bring to a boil. Add salt and pepper to taste and return the chicken pieces.
5. Cover and cook in the oven for about 1 hour or until the chicken is tender and cooked through.

Grilled Chicken Salad

A light chicken salad that is ideal for a summer picnic.

Season:
Summer

Cooking time:
20–30
minutes plus
chilling

2 large ripe tomatoes,
halved

½ cup/6 tbsp (90ml) olive oil

4 skinned chicken breast
fillets, about ¼ lb (100 g)
each

1 shallot, peeled and
chopped

4 tsp (20 ml) white wine
vinegar

2 tbsp (30 ml) half-and-half
(single cream)

1 tbsp (15 ml) chopped fresh
basil

salt and pepper to taste

mixed salad of lettuce,
tomatoes, olives, and green
(spring) onions, to serve

1. Broil the tomatoes until they are blackened,
   then purée them in a blender with a
   little of the olive oil until you've got a
   thin paste.

2. Lightly brush the chicken pieces with olive
   oil and broil, skinned-side down, for around
   8 minutes or until tender and cooked.

3. Turn the chicken pieces over, lightly brush
   them with the tomato paste, and broil (grill)
   them for a further 5 minutes or until the
   toppingis lightly browned. Cover and cool,
   then refrigerate for at least 1 hour.

4. Beat the shallot with the remaining olive
   oil, the vinegar, half-and-half (single cream),
   basil, and salt and pepper to taste.

5. Thinly slice the chicken and spoon the
   dressing over the chicken. Serve with
   the salad.

Duck Salad with Beans

This yang *salad makes a wonderfully refreshing lunch on a summer day.*

Season:
Summer

Cooking time: 15–25 minutes plus cooling

¼ lb (100 g) trimmed French beans

¼ lb (100 g) fresh lima beans

3 oz (75 g) watercress

1 orange, peeled and thinly sliced

½ cup/2 oz (50 g) black olives

4 duck breast fillets

1 tbsp (15 ml) olive oil

1 tbsp (15 ml) orange juice

salt and pepper to taste

1. Steam the beans until just tender, then transfer to a bowl and leave to cool.

2. Add the watercress, orange slices, and olives.

3. Immediately before serving, broil (grill) the duck lightly for about 4–5 minutes on each side, cut it into strips, and add to the salad.

4. Mix the oil and orange juice together, add salt and pepper to taste. Pour it over the salad before serving.

THE TAO OF FISH

There is a distinction between river fish and sea fish: river fish are generally more *yin* than their sea cousins which, because of the salt content, are more *yang*. However, both types are well balanced, falling between the extremes of *yin* and *yang*, though they do have a more *yang* quality than *yin*.

Fishing and the Tao

Fishing is a very Taoist pursuit. It involves accepting what is, being patient but still taking action, being a natural part of the world around you, enjoying yourself, relaxing and, of course, providing for yourself.

Ideally, fish should be cooked on the river bank as soon as they have been caught. If you can't do this, then any fish you buy should be as fresh as possible. (Frozen fish have a negative energy effect so shouldn't be used.) Probably the best way to buy fish is straight from the fishermen on the quayside as they bring the boats in just after dawn. The fish can then be taken straight home and lightly cooked and eaten as an appetizing breakfast.

How to Cook Fish

Small whole fish should simply be shallow-fried in a little butter and served plain. Dip them in a little flour first, if preferred, and turn once only so they are cooked on both sides.

Poaching is probably the best way to cook fish. Put the fish in a buttered flameproof dish or shallow pan with a little water or wine and bring gently to a boil. Cover with a lid and allow to simmer for only a few minutes until the flesh breaks away from any bones.

Yin and Yang Fish

The darker the fish (e.g. tuna), the more *yang* it is. The oilier the fish (e.g. mackerel), the more *yin* it is.

Deep-sea fish, such as cod, are more *yang* than shallow-feeding flat fish such as plaice and sole. Cold-water fish, such as herring and trout, are more *yin* than warm-water fish such as red snapper. All seafood is *yang* in essence, but crab, lobster, and other shellfish are fairly *yin* in nature.

Fish need to be cooked very lightly to retain their yang aspect as they can quickly and easily become too *yin*. If you overcook salmon, for example, you can cause quite considerable indigestion because of the breakdown in the *yang* energy.

Seafood and fish are a vital source of protein and are considered yang *by the Taoists. They should be eaten fresh from the ocean or river.*

"No wind, no waves"

Grilled Trout and Lentils

This is a light but warming supper dish; it incorporates Puy lentils, which are the small, dark lentils generally considered to be the best.

Season:
Spring

Cooking time:
35–45 minutes

1½ tbsp (25 ml) olive oil

1 onion, peeled and finely chopped

2 garlic cloves, peeled and sliced

1 cup/6 oz (175 g) Puy lentils

½ cup/6 tbsp (90 ml) vegetable stock (see page 55)

½ cup/6 tbsp (90 ml) white wine

salt and pepper to taste

juice of ½ lemon

4 rainbow trout fillets

1. Heat 1 tablespoon of oil in a skillet, add the onion and garlic, and fry for 5 minutes or until soft.
2. Add the lentils and stir thoroughly. Pour in the stock and wine and bring to a boil, then reduce the heat, cover and simmer for about 30 minutes or until the liquid has been absorbed. Add salt and pepper to taste.
3. Meanwhile, combine the remaining oil with the lemon juice and brush over the fish.
4. When the lentils have been cooking for about 20 minutes, cook the fish under the broiler for about 4 minutes on each side.
5. Serve the fish with the lentils.

Salmon and Spinach Pasta

This satisfying meal is packed with natural vitamins and minerals. Its colorful appearance suggests a good balance between yin *and* yang.

Season:
Summer

Cooking time:
10–15 minutes

¾ lb (350 g) fresh tagliatelle

½ cup/6 tbsp (90 ml) olive oil

1 onion, peeled and finely chopped

6 oz (175 g) zucchini (courgettes), cut into batons

¾ lb (350 g) spinach, roughly chopped

¾ lb (350 g) fresh salmon, cooked and flaked

juice of 1 lemon

salt and pepper to taste

1. Cook the fresh pasta in boiling water for about 8 minutes or until tender.
2. Meanwhile, heat the oil in a skillet, add the onion, and fry for about 5 minutes or until soft.
3. Add the zucchini (courgettes) and cook for about 2 minutes, then add the spinach and cook for a few minutes more, or until the spinach has wilted. Stir in the fish and lemon juice.
4. When the pasta is cooked, drain it and toss it with the salmon and spinach mixture. Add salt and pepper to taste, and serve.

Fish and Cheese Pie

This is a delicious and filling dish which can be served with potatoes and a green vegetable such as broccoli or cabbage.

Season:
Fall

Cooking time:
35–45
minutes

1½ lb (750 g) haddock or cod fillets

2½ cups/1 pint (600 ml) milk

4 tbsp/2 oz (50 g) butter

good ½ cup/2 oz (50 g) plain flour

½ lb (225 g) medium flavor hard cheese, e.g. Cheddar, grated

salt and pepper to taste

4 tomatoes, sliced

1. Preheat the oven to 350°F, 180°C, gas mark 4.

2. Poach the fish in the milk in a shallow pan for about 10 minutes or until just cooked. Transfer the fish to a pie dish, reserving the milk.

3. Melt the butter in a saucepan, stirring in the flour and cook for 1 minute. Remove from the heat and add the poaching milk, a little at a time, stirring continuously to prevent lumps forming.

4. When all the milk has been added, add all but 2–3 tbsp (30–45 g) of the grated cheese and stir in. Bring to a boil, stirring continuously, then taste and add salt and pepper.

5. Pour the cheese sauce over the fish and lay the tomato slices on top to cover it. Top with the reserved grated cheese.

6. Bake in the oven for around 20 minutes. Serve hot.

"When you want to test the depths of a stream, don't use both feet"

Cider-baked Mackerel

A very tasty lunchtime dish for when mackerel is in season –
preferably caught locally – and the cider is fresh.

● Season:
Fall

⏱ Cooking time:
50–60
minutes

⅓ cup/4 tbsp (60 ml) cider

1 onion, peeled and sliced

1 bay leaf

sprig of parsley

sprig of thyme

6 peppercorns

pinch of salt

4 good-sized fresh mackerel,
cleaned

⅔ cup/5 oz (150 g) plain
yogurt

1 tsp (5 ml) muscovado
sugar

1 tbsp (15 ml) chopped herb
fennel

lemon wedges, to garnish

1. Preheat the oven to 350°F, 180°C,
   gas mark 4.
2. Put ¼ cup/3 tbsp (45 ml) cider into a large
   shallow pan with 1¼ cups/½ pint (300 ml)
   water, the onion, herbs, peppercorns, and
   salt. Bring to a boil, then reduce the heat
   and simmer for about 20 minutes.
3. Put the mackerel into a shallow ovenproof
   dish and pour the liquid over it. Cover and
   cook in the oven for around 25 minutes.
4. Transfer the fish to a warmed serving
   dish and keep hot.
5. Put the yogurt, sugar, remaining cider, and
   fennel into a small heatproof bowl and place
   over a pan of simmering water. Blend the
   sauce ingredients well and pour it over the
   fish. Garnish with lemon wedges, serve hot.

Roast Salmon with Mustard

A very light, but yang, *dish that is refreshing on a warmish winter day when nothing too heavy or filling is required.*

Season:
Winter

Cooking time:
20–30
minutes

2½ lb (1.1 kg) boned middle cut of salmon

¾ cup/6 oz (175 g) butter, melted

¼ cup/3 tbsp (45 ml) whole grain mustard

4 tsp (20 ml) chopped dill

salt and pepper to taste

11 oz (300 g) fresh spinach

1. Preheat the oven to 450°F, 230°C, gas mark 8.
2. Cut and open out the salmon and place, skin-side up, in a shallow ovenproof dish.
3. Blend the butter, mustard, dill, and salt and pepper to taste. Spread over the salmon and cook in the oven for about 20 minutes.
4. Meanwhile, very lightly cook the spinach in a little water, and drain. Arrange the spinach on serving plates. Cut the salmon into thick slices and serve on top of the spinach. Spoon the mustard butter over the top. Serve hot.

Fish Stew

A marvelously warming yang *dish to beat the damp winter chills. The fish included in this recipe should come straight from the sea.*

Season:
Winter

Cooking time:
40–50
minutes

pinch of saffron strands

½ cup/6 tbsp (90 ml) olive oil

2 large onions, peeled and chopped

4 cloves garlic, peeled and chopped

1 red pepper, seeded and thinly sliced

2 lb (900 g) tomatoes, chopped

1¼ cups/½ pint (300 ml) white wine

½ cup/6 tbsp (90 ml) chopped basil

4 bay leaves

4 lb (1.8 kg) mixed fish, such as plaice, red mullet, cod, and monkfish

salt and pepper to taste

24 peeled cooked prawns

5 oz (150 g) cooked mussels, shelled

8 slices of toast

1. Pour a little boiling water over the saffron strands in a cup or small bowl, and leave for around 30 minutes.
2. Meanwhile, heat the oil in a saucepan, add the onions, garlic, and red pepper, and fry for about 5 minutes.
3. Add the tomatoes and stir well. Add the wine and 1¼ cups of water.
4. Bring to a boil, then reduce the heat, add the bay leaves and basil. Simmer for 20 minutes.
5. Cut the fish into chunks. Add the firm fish to the saucepan with the saffron water and salt and pepper to taste. Cook for 10 minutes.
6. Add the soft fish, prawns, and mussels, and cook for another 5 minutes or so.
7. Remove the bay leaves from the stew, cover and keep warm.
8. Cut the toast into croûtons and line four large soup bowls with them. Spoon over the stew and serve hot.

Tuna Steaks with Basil Butter

A light, refreshing summer lunch that is quick to cook, though it does need a little time to prepare.

● **Season:**
Summer

Ⓙ **Cooking time:**
15–25
minutes plus
marinating

**4 tuna steaks, about 6 oz
(175 g) each**

½ cup/6 tbsp (90 ml) olive oil

**2 cloves garlic, peeled and
crushed**

**2 tsp (10 ml) balsamic
vinegar**

**2 tbsp (30 ml) chopped
herbs, such as thyme and
parsley**

salt and pepper to taste

**6 tbsp/3 oz (75g) unsalted
butter, melted**

**2 tbsp freshly grated
Parmesan cheese**

1 tsp (15 ml) sherry vinegar

**6 fresh basil leaves, finely
shredded**

fresh herbs, to garnish

1. Place the tuna steaks into a shallow ovenproof dish.

2. Beat together the olive oil, garlic, balsamic vinegar, herbs, and salt and pepper to taste, and pour the dressing over the tuna steaks. Coat well and leave to marinate in the refrigerator for 3 hours.

3. Blend the butter with the Parmesan cheese, sherry vinegar, and basil leaves.

4. Take the steaks from the refrigerator and place under the broiler. Cook for 12–15 minutes or until tender, brushing well with Parmesan butter. Serve at once with a fresh herb garnish.

Grilled Lobster

A quick, light, summer lunch ideal for eating outdoors on a hot summer's day.

● **Season:**
Summer

Ⓙ **Cooking time:**
5–10
minutes

**4 cooked lobsters, each
about 1 lb (450 g)**

salt and pepper to taste

**4 tbsp/2 oz (50 g) butter,
melted**

lemon wedge, to garnish

1. Remove the meat from the lobster including from inside the claws. Sprinkle the flesh with a little salt and pepper and brush with melted butter.

2. Cook under a broiler set to medium for about 5 minutes.

3. Serve on a warmed plate with lemon wedges as a garnish.

Prawn and Potato Salad

This dish uses seasonal potatoes and fresh prawns which should be added just before serving.

Season:
Summer

Cooking time:
35–45 minutes plus cooling

1 lb (450 g) new potatoes

2 handfuls fresh mint

1 lb (450 g) shelled lima beans

¾ cup/6 oz (175 g) plain yogurt

⅔ cup/¼ pint (150 ml) mayonnaise

salt and pepper to taste

½ lb (225 g) peeled cooked prawns

1. Cook the potatoes in boiling water with half the mint for about 25 minutes. Drain and leave to cool.

2. Steam the beans until tender, then let them cool. Slice the potatoes and add to the beans.

3. Finely chop the remaining mint and add this to the yogurt and mayonnaise. Mix together thoroughly.

4. Stir the potatoes and beans into this mixture and add salt and pepper to taste.

5. Immediately before serving, stir in the prawns.

Flounder or Plaice Veronique

A light fall dish that is well balanced between yin *and* yang, *and is refreshing but substantial.*

Season:
Fall

Cooking time:
15–25
minutes

6 oz (175 g) seedless green grapes

8 large flounder (plaice) fillets, each about ¼ lb (100 g), skinned

½ cup/6 tbsp (90 ml) white wine

½ cup/6 tbsp (90 ml) fish stock

2 tsp (10 ml) finely chopped basil

4 bay leaves

1 tsp (5 ml) cornstarch (cornflour)

½ cup/6 tbsp (90 ml) milk

salt and pepper to taste

2 tbsp (30ml) Greek yogurt

1. Put four grapes on each flounder fillet, roll up and secure with a toothpick. Put all the flounder (plaice) fillets in a large poaching pan.

2. Mix together the wine, stock, basil, and bay leaves, and pour over the flounder (plaice).

3. Bring to a boil, then reduce the heat, cover and simmer for 10 minutes or until the fish is cooked. Remove the fish from the pan with a slotted spoon. Remove the toothpicks and bay leaves, and keep warm.

4. Mix the cornstarch (cornflour) with the milk and stir into the cooking liquid in the pan. Add salt and pepper to taste and bring to a boil, stirring, until the liquid thickens. Simmer for about 5 minutes.

5. Stir in the yogurt, add the remaining grapes, and pour over the flounder (plaice) fillets.

Roast Monkfish with Bacon and Sweet Potatoes

A delicious fall lunch for when the weather is starting to get cold and you need something to warm you and keep the damp out.

Season:
Fall

Cooking time:
45–55
minutes

1½ lb (750 g) monkfish fillets

8 strips smoked fatty (streaky) bacon

juice of ½ lemon

salt and pepper to taste

1½ lb (750 g) sweet potatoes, scrubbed

2 red onions, peeled and chopped

12 cloves garlic, peeled

2 sprigs rosemary

¼ cup/4 tbsp (60 ml) olive oil

8 oz (225 g) small tomatoes

1. Preheat the oven to 450°F, 230°C, gas mark 8.

2. Wash and dry the monkfish, and cut into four large pieces. Wrap each piece in two strips of bacon. Drizzle over the lemon juice and sprinkle with a little salt and pepper to taste.

3. Cut the sweet potatoes into wedges and place in a large roasting pan with the onions, garlic, and rosemary sprigs. Sprinkle with salt and pepper to taste, and stir in the olive oil. Roast in the oven for about 15 minutes.

4. Remove the pan from the oven and arrange the monkfish pieces among the vegetables. Make sure some vegetables are on top to cover them. Roast for 30 minutes or until the fish is tender and cooked through.

5. Serve hot with the tomatoes.

"No one can see their reflection in running water. It is only in still water that we can see"

THE TAO OF RICE

Both rice and Taoism traditionally have been seen as Chinese but they have spread throughout the world. It is no coincidence that they go together, the Chinese have the same word for both – *tao* – which also, interestingly, means a road or path; to go through fire and water (which is what rice has to do); and also change or to be fluid and adaptable.

While this is a book about the Taoist approach to food and not about Chinese cooking, it is interesting to explore the ways the Chinese cook and prepare rice.

There are three basic methods that the Chinese use:

1 SOFT RICE. This is made by boiling rice in water for about one-and-a-half-hours. You need about eight times as much water as rice. Soft rice is known as "congee" and is served as a breakfast with a strong-tasting food such as ham, or sweetened to make a pudding.

2 STEAMED RICE. You will need about two and a half times the amount of water to rice, and a bamboo steamer. The rice is washed and put into the steamer which is then placed over a boiling pan of water. If you haven't got a steamer, then put the rice in the boiling water, immediately turn down the heat and cover the saucepan with a lid. Leave the rice to steam in its own heat until cooked. Steamed rice is served at lunch and with an evening meal, and it is the staple diet of most Chinese even today.

3 SOLID RICE. This is prepared in the same way as congee, but with more water and using round-grain rice. When it is cooked it is dried and turned into rice cakes which are eaten as a snack. Solid rice is often used as a basis for a cake mixture into which dried fruit, nuts, and spices are added, not dissimilar to the traditional rice pudding in the West, but a lot more solid and dry.

Fried rice, which many think of as being Chinese, isn't actually. It is a Western invention to use up leftover rice and although it is served in Chinese restaurants it wouldn't be served in China, except occasionally as a quick snack for hungry children.

Types of Rice

You might like to try experimenting with different types of rice. They include Basmati, which is a long-grain rice with a naturally aromatic smell and flavor from the foothills of the Himalayas in India. You could also try Italian rice, known as "piemontese" or "arborio" rice, which is excellent for risotto. Patna rice is a long-grain, naturally white, rice which cooks to a very dry consistency making it good for pilaffs and rice salads. For puddings try Java rice; this is a short version of a long-grain rice and cooks up very fluffy. Wild rice isn't rice at all but a closely related aquatic grass seed from the United States, but its distinctive nutty taste makes it a useful and interesting alternative.

Washing Rice

Whichever rice you choose the important thing to do is not to wash it too much. We are taught in the West that we have to wash rice thoroughly, but it isn't a good thing to do. The outer covering of rice contains a lot of vitamin B which is essential for good health. Washing rice depletes this useful vitamin.

Fried Rice

Rice is often served as an accompaniment; fried rice is one of the most tasty Chinese rice dishes.

● **Season:**
Summer

🕐 **Cooking time:**
5–10
minutes

2 tbsp (30 ml) vegetable oil

3 green (spring) onions chopped

¼ lb (100 g) button mushrooms

3 eggs, beaten

⅓ cup/2 oz (50 g) diced, lean cooked ham

⅓ cup/2 oz (50 g) peeled fresh shrimp

2½ cups/6 oz (175 g) cooked long-grain brown rice

1. Heat the oil in a wok or skillet, add the green onions and mushrooms, and cook for 30 seconds.
2. Reduce the heat and add the eggs. Cook until lightly scrambled, then transfer to a warm dish.
3. Put the ham, shrimp, and rice into the skillet and stir-fry for about 2 minutes.
4. Return the scrambled egg to the pan and cook for a further minute.
5. Serve immediately.

Apple Rice

This is an unusual and refreshing variation on the traditional Chinese rice accompaniment.

Season: Winter

Cooking time: 50–60 minutes

2 tbsp (30 ml) vegetable oil

1 large cooking apple, peeled, cored, and sliced

1 onion, finely chopped

1 good cup/½ lb (225 g) long-grain brown rice

1 tsp (5 ml) ground cumin

2½ cups/1 pint (600 ml) vegetable stock (see page 55)

1. Heat the oil in a pan and fry the apple and onion gently for about 5 minutes, or until beginning to soften.
2. Add the rice and cumin and stir for 1 minute, then pour in the stock and bring to a boil.
3. Reduce the heat, cover and simmer for 35–40 minutes or until the liquid is absorbed and the rice is tender.
4. Let stand, covered, for 5 minutes before serving.

"Learning is a treasure that will follow its owner everywhere"

Herb Rice

This summery rice goes well with vegetables and is excellent served cold.

Vegan

Season: Summer

Cooking time: 35–45 minutes

1 good cup/½ lb (225 g) long-grain brown rice

¼ tsp (1.25 ml) sea salt

2 tbsp (30 ml) finely chopped parsley

2 tbsp (30 ml) finely chopped mint

2 tbsp (30 ml) finely chopped chives

2 tbsp (30 ml) finely chopped tarragon

ground black pepper to taste

1. Rinse the rice well and put in a saucepan with 2½ cups/1 pint (600 ml) cold water. Bring to a boil, then turn the heat down very low, cover, and cook until the rice is tender and the water is completely absorbed.
2. Add all the herbs and stir. Add black pepper to taste and serve hot or cold.

Spicy Rice

An excellent vegan rice dish that is easy to prepare. It makes a good accompaniment to braised vegetable dishes such as ratatouille.

Vegan

Season:
Winter

Cooking time:
25–35
minutes

1 good cup/½ lb (225 g) basmati rice

1 bay leaf

½ stick cinnamon

3 cardamom pods, crushed

1 tsp (5 ml) cumin seeds

¼ tsp (1.25 ml) sea salt

ground black pepper to taste

1. Rinse the rice well and put into a saucepan with 2½ cups/1 pint (600 ml) cold water. Add the bay leaf, spices, and salt, and bring to a boil.
2. Turn the heat down low, cover and simmer for about 20 minutes or until the rice is tender and all the water is absorbed.
3. Add black pepper to taste and serve hot or leave to cool.

Lemon Rice

A refreshing spring rice dish to chase away the winter blues as well as any lingering illnesses.

Vegan

Season:
Spring

Cooking time:
45–55
minutes

1 good cup/½ lb (225 g) long-grain brown rice

¼ tsp (1.25 ml) sea salt

grated or finely pared zest and juice of ½ lemon

ground black pepper to taste

1. Rinse the rice and put into a saucepan with 2½ cups/1 pint (600 ml) cold water and the salt. Bring to a boil, then lower the heat, cover and simmer for about 40 minutes or until the rice is tender and all the water is absorbed.
2. Add the lemon zest and juice, and stir well. Add black pepper to taste and serve hot or cold.

Fruit and Nut Risotto

Rice is the most basic Taoist food; here it is mixed with simple, fresh, and energy-giving ingredients.

Vegan

● **Season:**
Fall

Ⓙ **Cooking time:**
10–20 minutes plus soaking

6 oz (175 g) dried apricots or apples, or a mixture of both

1 tsp (5 ml) pure cooking oil

1 onion, peeled and finely chopped

3 cups/½ lb (225 g) cooked brown rice

1 tsp (5 ml) ground allspice

salt and pepper to taste

½ cup/3 oz (75 g) raisins

½ cup/2 oz (50 g) flaked almonds

1. Place the dried apricots or apples in a bowl, cover with water, and leave to soak for about 4 hours.
2. Drain the soaked fruit and chop it roughly.
3. Heat the oil in a pan, add the onion, and cook for about 5 minutes, or until soft.
4. Stir the cooked rice into the pan with the allspice and salt and pepper to taste, and stir until heated through.
5. Add the fruit and nuts, and heat for a further 3–4 minutes before serving.

Chicken Risotto

This is an excellent dish for late fall, to help stock up energy for the coming winter.

● **Season:**
Fall

Ⓙ **Cooking time:**
1–1¼ hours

2 tbsp (30 ml) olive oil

1 leek, cut into chunks

½ cup/2 oz (50 g) quartered mushrooms

1 good cup/½ lb (225 g) long-grain brown rice

1½ cups/12 fl oz (350 ml) chicken stock (see page 55)

3 oz (75 g) green beans, finely sliced

1⅓ cups/½ lb (225 g) cooked chicken, cut into bite-sized pieces

2 tbsp (30 ml) whole almonds

salt and pepper to taste

½ lb (225 g) plain yogurt

1. Heat the oil in a deep saucepan, add the leek, and fry gently until soft.
2. Add the mushrooms and cook for about 2 minutes. Add the rice and stir for a further 2 minutes or so. Add the stock and bring to a boil, stirring continuously, then reduce the heat and simmer for about 40 minutes, or until the rice is tender and the liquid has been absorbed.
3. Steam the beans until just tender, and add to the rice. Add the chicken and almonds, and cook for another 2 minutes to heat through. Taste, and add salt and pepper if required.
4. Serve hot, accompanied by plain yogurt.

Mushroom and Nut Risotto

This is a simple rice dish that can be served alone or as an accompaniment to meat or fish.

Season:
Winter

Cooking time:
50–60
minutes

2 tbsp (30 ml) olive oil

1 small onion, peeled and chopped

1 stalk celery, chopped

1 head of Belgian endive (chicory), chopped

4 cups/½ lb (225 g) chopped mushrooms

¾ cup/6 oz (175 g) long-grain brown rice

⅔ cup/¼ pint (150 ml) white wine

⅔ cup/¼ pint (150 ml) vegetable stock (see page 55)

juice of ½ lemon

3 tbsp cashew nuts

salt and pepper to taste

1. Heat the oil in a large, shallow pan, add the onion, celery, endive (chicory), and mushrooms, and cook for about 5 minutes or until soft.
2. Add the rice and cook for around 2 minutes. Add the wine and stock, and bring to a boil, stirring, then reduce the heat and simmer for about 40 minutes or until the rice is tender and the liquid has been absorbed.
3. Add the lemon juice, nuts, and salt and pepper to taste, and serve.

Rice and Cheese Soufflé

This dish is very light because the egg whites cause it to rise; it doesn't waste the egg yolks but incorporates them as well.

Season:
Winter

Cooking time:
30–40
minutes

1½ cups/6 oz (175 g) finely grated medium-flavor hard cheese, e.g. Cheddar

1 good cup/½ lb (225 g) cooked long-grain brown rice

½ medium onion, peeled and grated

1 tsp (5 ml) ground cilantro (coriander)

1 tsp (5 ml) ground cumin

salt and pepper to taste

2 large or 3 small eggs, separated

a little milk

1. Preheat the oven to 375°F, 190°C, gas mark 5. Grease a soufflé dish.
2. Mix the cheese, rice, onion, spices, and salt and pepper in a bowl.
3. Add the egg yolks and mix well, adding a little milk if the mixture is too stiff to stir.
4. Beat the egg whites until very stiff and fold them carefully into the mixture.
5. Ease the mixture gently into the greased soufflé dish and bake in the oven for about 35 minutes, or until well risen and lightly browned. Remove from the oven and serve at once.

Nuts, rice, grains, and pulses are essential to our diet; they are a source of fiber and offer a balanced, staple yin/yang food.

Fried Rice Rissoles

This dish can be specially prepared, but it is also a good way to use up any rice left over from a previous meal.

Season:
Fall

Cooking time:
10–20 minutes

⅓ cup/4 tbsp (60 ml) vegetable oil

1 onion, peeled and finely chopped

scant 2 cups/¼ lb (100 g) cooked long-grain brown rice

ground hazelnuts

1 cup/¼ lb (100 g) grated cheese

½ tsp (2.5 ml) chopped fresh herb in season, e.g. sage, thyme, oregano

salt and pepper to taste

1 egg, beaten

¾ cup/2 oz (50 g) dry bread crumbs

1. Heat 1 tbsp oil in a skillet, add the onion, and fry for about 5 minutes or until tender.
2. Stir the onion into the rice with the nuts, cheese, herbs, and salt and pepper to taste.
3. Shape the mixture into rissoles. Dip in beaten egg and then coat with bread crumbs.
4. Heat the remaining oil in the skillet and fry the rissoles until golden brown and heated through.

Vegetable Pilau Rice

This makes a good accompaniment to any meat dish, or can be eaten on its own as a vegetarian meal.

Vegan

Season:
Winter

Cooking time:
30–40 minutes plus standing

1 good cup/½ lb (225 g) basmati rice

2 tbsp (30 ml) olive oil

½ tsp (2.5 ml) cumin seeds

2 bay leaves

4 green cardamom pods

4 cloves

1 onion, peeled and finely chopped

1 carrot, peeled and finely chopped

½ cup/2 oz (50 g) fresh podded peas

½ cup/2 oz (50 g) fresh corn kernels (sweetcorn), sliced off the husk

¼ cup/1 oz (25 g) cashew nuts, lightly fried

¼ tsp (1.25 ml) ground cumin

salt and pepper to taste

1. Wash the rice several times, put it into a bowl and cover with water. Leave to soak for 30 minutes.
2. Meanwhile, heat the oil in a large skillet and fry the cumin seeds for 2 about minutes. Add the bay leaves, cardamoms, and cloves, and fry for a further 2 minutes or so.
3. Add the onion to the pan and fry for about 5 minutes. Add the carrot and cook for a further 5 minutes or so.
4. Drain the rice and add it to the pan with the peas, corn, and cashew nuts. Fry for around 5 minutes.
5. Add 2 cups/16 fl oz (475 ml) water and the remaining spices with salt and pepper to taste. Bring to a boil, then reduce the heat, cover and simmer over a low heat for 15 minutes or until all the water is absorbed.
6. Leave to stand, covered, for about 10 minutes before serving.

Rice and Mushroom Pancakes

*A wonderfully warming vegetarian rice dish to combat
the onset of fall.*

Vegetarian

Season:
Fall

**Cooking
time:**
1¼–1½
hours

**1 good cup/½ lb (225 g)
long-grain brown rice**

**⅓ cup/4 tbsp (60 ml) olive
oil**

**3 cups/11 oz (300 g) sliced
mushrooms**

**2 onions, peeled and
chopped**

1 cup/¼ lb (100 g) plain flour

**½ cup/6 tbsp (90 ml) heavy
(double) cream**

½ cup/6 tbsp (90 ml) milk

2 large eggs

**½ tsp (2.5 ml) grated
nutmeg**

**a little salt and pepper
to taste**

**2 cloves garlic, peeled and
crushed**

**1 lb (450 g) tomatoes,
chopped**

½ tsp (2.5 ml) caster sugar

**2 tbsp (30 ml) chopped
fresh basil**

fresh basil, to garnish

1. Rinse the rice and put into a saucepan with
   2½ cups/1 pint (600 ml) cold water. Bring to
   a boil, then reduce the heat, cover and
   simmer for about 40 minutes, or until the
   rice is tender and the water absorbed.

2. Heat 1 tbsp (15 ml) olive oil in a skillet, add
   the mushrooms and half the onion, and
   cook for 7–8 minutes.

3. Blend the flour, cream, milk, eggs, and
   nutmeg together in a bowl. Add salt and
   pepper, and stir in the mushrooms and rice.

4. Heat 1 tbsp (15 ml) olive oil in the skillet,
   add the remaining onion and the garlic, and
   cook for about 3 minutes.

5. Add the tomatoes, sugar, and water. Bring to
   the boil, then reduce the heat and simmer
   for around 10 minutes. Add the basil and
   salt and pepper to taste.

6. Heat the remaining oil in another skillet.
   Spoon in about ⅓ cup/4 tbsp (60 ml) of the
   rice pancake mixture and cook for 2–3
   minutes on each side. Repeat to make eight
   pancakes in total. Garnish with a little basil
   and serve with the tomato sauce and a
   accompany with a fresh salad.

> "Listen to all,
> plucking a
> feather from
> every passing
> goose, but
> follow no one
> absolutely"

Nutty Rice Salad

A quick winter rice dish that is excellent for nutrition and warmth.
This dish is also good for vegans.

Vegan

Season:
Winter

Cooking time:
40–50
minutes

¾ cup/6 oz (175 g) long-grain brown rice

¾ cup/3 oz (75 g) toasted and chopped hazelnuts

1 red pepper, seeded and sliced

10 green onions, sliced

4 stalks celery, sliced

⅔ cup/2 oz (50 g) sliced button mushrooms

3 tbsp (45 ml) chopped parsley

1. Rinse the rice well and put into a saucepan with 2½ cups/1 pint (600 ml) cold water. Bring to the boil,
   then reduce the heat, cover and simmer for about 40 minutes or until the rice is tender and the water absorbed. Rinse and drain well.

2. Add all the remaining ingredients to the rice and mix thoroughly.

3. Serve warm or cold.

Rice Cakes

These can be served with a dip or as an accompaniment to soup.

Season:
All

Cooking time:
25–35
minutes plus
overnight
drying

¾ cup/6 oz (175 g) long-grain white rice

vegetable oil to grease tray and for deep frying

1. Wash the rice and put it into a saucepan with 1½ cups/12 fl oz (350 ml) water, cover, and bring to a boil, then reduce the heat and simmer, still covered, for about 15 minutes, or until the water is absorbed and the rice is tender.

2. Fluff the rice with a fork and turn it out onto a lightly greased baking sheet. Press flat with a large spoon.

3. Leave to dry out overnight in a very low oven, 225°F, 110°C, gas mark ¼.

4. Break up the baked rice into wafer-sized pieces to make individual rice cakes.

5. Heat the oil and deep-fry the rice cakes for about 1 minute, or until they puff up. Drain and serve, or cool and store in an airtight container.

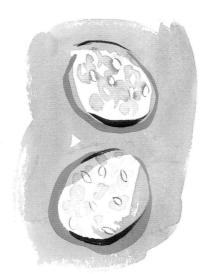

Tao is the Chinese w
for rice, a food that
staple part of the
Chinese diet.

THE TAO OF VEGETABLES AND SALADS

Vegetables

Technically, a vegetable is any plant – something that is not animal. However, we generally use the term to mean carrots and the like. We also tend to refer to the vegetables that grow beneath the surface of the ground as "root" vegetables. All plants are, by their very nature *yin*, but those which grow with the part we eat below the ground are even more so.

Yin Qualities

Invariably, you can eat vegetables raw if you choose to do so, but remember that this preserves their *yin* qualities to an even greater extent. This can be advantageous – raw vegetables taken from the ground and eaten immediately provide a massive burst of cooling *yin* energy if you need it to combat the *yang* heat of summer.

Cooking Vegetables

When cooked, vegetables lose some of their *yin* essence and become slightly more *yang*. The longer they are cooked, the more *yang* they become. This is why vegetables spoil if cooked for too long — they lose their *yin* qualities and degenerate into a soggy *yang* mess, which is not their natural condition. Vegetables should be very lightly steamed to preserve their *yin* energy.

PULSES

Pulses – such as beans, peas, and lentils – are the seeds of leguminous plants. "Leguminous" means that the seeds grow in a pod, so although they may grow above the ground they still grow in the dark *yin*. So they too can be eaten raw and still have enormous taste and flavor. You can, of course, buy dried beans and peas, but fresh is best. Lentils are invariably dried and need soaking, but you could try growing your own.

Pulsating Energy

"Pulses" may mean "seeds" but they also "pulsate" with energy, and that energy is very *yin*. Too much raw food is not especially good for you or your digestion; the *ch'i* energy released is very cooling and can make you feel cut off from reality. It is better to steam vegetables lightly to reduce their *yin* qualities and add a little warming *yang* to them before eating. This aids the digestion and relieves any discomfort that excess wind might generate. In the *yang* summer heat, however, vegetables such as carrots, and pulses such as beans, are best eaten raw in salads for their cooling attributes. You should always have a little *yang* meat with your salad though, to counteract the excessive *yin* food. Cold-cooked meat loses some of its *yang* qualities so it harmonizes well. If you are going to serve cold meat, make sure it is very fresh.

"Make happy those who are near and those who are far will come"

Root Vegetable Casserole

You can adapt this recipe to use the freshest vegetables in season.

Season:
Winter

Cooking time:
30–40
minutes

2 lb (900 g) fresh mixed root
vegetables, e.g. carrots,
parsnips, sweet potatoes,
rutabaga (swede), turnips,
potatoes

3 cups/1½ pints (750 ml)
vegetable stock
(see page 55)

2 tsp (10 ml) chopped fresh
herbs in season, e.g.
rosemary, sage, thyme

salt and pepper to taste

1. Peel and cube the vegetables, place in a large saucepan, and cover with the stock.
2. Bring to a boil, then reduce the heat, and simmer for about 25 minutes.
3. Add the herbs and continue to simmer for a further 5 minutes or so.
4. Add salt and pepper to taste, and serve.

Celery, Bean, and Green Onion Stew

This is an excellent dish for restoring energy after the winter. It can be served as a main course or a side dish.

Season:
Spring

Cooking time:
20–30
minutes

¼ cup/3 tbsp (45 ml)
vegetable oil

4 small hearts of celery,
sliced

½ lb (225 g) fresh beans

4 bunches green (spring)
onions, finely chopped

1½ cups/12 fl oz (350 ml)
white wine

salt and pepper to taste

1. Heat the oil in a saucepan, add the celery, and cook gently for 5 minutes or until soft.
2. Add the remaining ingredients, except the salt and pepper, and bring to a boil. Reduce the heat, cover and simmer for 15 minutes.
4. Add salt and pepper to taste, and serve.

Artichoke and Brussels Sprout Purée

This is a warming dish best served at an evening meal to accompany roast meat.

Season:
Winter

Cooking time:
10–15 minutes

1½ lb (750 g) Jerusalem artichokes

1½ lb (750 g) prepared Brussels sprouts

1 oz (25 g) butter

1 tsp (5 ml) freshly grated nutmeg

salt and pepper to taste

knob of butter, to serve

1. Peel and roughly chop the artichokes. Steam with the sprouts until tender.

2. Transfer the vegetables to a bowl, add the butter and nutmeg, and mash to a purée.

3. Add salt and pepper to taste, and serve with a knob of butter.

Carrots in Orange Sauce

This side dish is tastiest if you use young, fresh carrots. It also adds refreshing color to your plate.

● **Season:**
Fall

⏱ **Cooking time:**
25–35
minutes

1 lb (450 g) young carrots, scrubbed and sliced

1½ tbsp/¾ oz (20 g) butter

3 tbsp/¾ oz (20 g) plain wholemeal flour

juice of 2 oranges

2 tbsp (30 ml) half-and-half (single cream)

salt and pepper to taste

1. Put the carrots into a saucepan and cover with water. Bring to a boil and cook for about 20 minutes, or until tender.
2. Meanwhile, melt the butter in a saucepan and stir in the flour. Remove from the heat and stir in the orange juice and half-and-half (single cream), beating with a spoon to prevent lumps forming.
3. When the carrots are cooked, drain them and reserve a good ¾ cup/7 oz (200 ml) of the cooking water. Add this water to the orange and half-and-half (single cream) mixture, stirring well. Bring the sauce slowly to a boil, stirring constantly, to thicken.
4. Add salt and pepper to taste to the sauce, pour it over the carrots, and serve.

Beet Salad

Delicious as an accompaniment or on its own, this dish is quick to prepare.

Vegetarian

○ **Season:**
Spring

⏱ **Preparation time:**
15–25
minutes plus chilling

1 lb (450 g) raw baby beets (beetroot)

2 tbsp (30 ml) raspberry vinegar

¼ tsp (1.25 ml) clear honey

1 clove garlic, peeled and crushed

1 tbsp (15 ml) grated fresh horseradish

scant ½ cup/3 fl oz (75 ml) walnut oil

2 tbsp (30 ml) olive oil

salt and pepper to taste

½ small red onion, peeled and thinly sliced

2 tbsp chopped fresh chives

1. Peel the beets and set aside.
2. Beat together the vinegar, honey, garlic, horseradish, and oil. Add salt and pepper to taste.
3. Cut the beets in halves and grate finely. Stir the dressing into the beets. Add the onion and chives. Chill for around 1 hour and serve cold.

Carrot and Parsnip au Gratin

A delicious hot vegetable dish, ideal on a cold fall day to warm you and fill you up.

Vegan

Season:
Fall

Cooking time:
30–40 minutes plus cooling

1 lb (450 g) carrots, peeled and chopped

1 lb (450 g) parsnips, peeled and chopped

2½ cups/1 pint (600 ml) vegetable stock (see page 55)

salt and pepper to taste

1 cup/2 oz (50 g) fresh bread crumbs

olive oil (optional)

chopped fresh parsley, to garnish

1. Put the carrots and parsnips into a large saucepan with the stock and salt and pepper to taste. Bring to a boil, then reduce the heat, cover, and simmer gently for 20 minutes, or until the vegetables are tender and well cooked. Drain and leave to cool.

2. Mash the vegetables to a smooth purée and spread in a heatproof dish. Sprinkle with bread crumbs and broil under a hot grill until the top turns brown. You might like to brush the top with a little olive oil.

3. Serve hot, garnished with parsley.

Ginger Squash

Come in from the garden on a cold fall day to a dish of Ginger Squash and you'll feel revived in seconds.

Vegetarian

Season:
Fall

Cooking time:
15–25 minutes

3 lb (1.4 kg) butternut squash, seeded, peeled, and cut into chunks

1 stick/¼ lb (100 g) butter

2 cups/¼ lb (100 g) fresh bread crumbs

1 inch piece of fresh root ginger, peeled and sliced

2 cloves garlic, peeled and crushed

⅓ cup/2 oz (50 g) pine nuts

¼ cup/4 tbsp (60 ml) chopped fresh parsley

salt and pepper to taste

1. Cook the pieces of squash in boiling water for 15 minutes, or until just tender. Drain and keep warm.

2. Melt the butter in a large skillet and add the bread crumbs, ginger, garlic, and pine nuts. Fry for 5 minutes or until the bread crumbs are golden brown.

3. Add the parsley to the bread crumb mixture and add salt and pepper to taste. Stir in the squash pieces and serve warm.

"Without rice, even the cleverest housewife cannot cook"

Zucchini Salad

This will serve four as a side salad, or two as a main dish.

Season:
Summer

Cooking time:
1–5 minutes,
plus
marinating

4 zucchini (courgettes),
peeled and diced

1 onion, peeled and finely
chopped

1 clove garlic, peeled and
crushed

2 tomatoes, skinned and
finely chopped

½ green pepper, seeded and
finely chopped

2 tbsp (30 ml) olive oil

juice of 1 lemon

1 tsp (5 ml) chopped basil

salt and pepper to taste

1. Blanch the zucchini (courgettes) in boiling water for around 1 minute. Drain well.

2. Mix the zucchini (courgettes) with the onion, garlic, tomatoes, and green pepper. Stir in the olive oil, lemon juice, and basil, and leave to marinate for about 1 hour.

3. Add salt and pepper to taste, and serve.

Avocado and Strawberry Salad

This unusual combination provides a refreshing, light side salad to accompany a meal on a hot day.

Season:
Summer

Preparation time:
10–20 minutes

2 ripe avocados

12 strawberries, hulled

juice of 1 lemon

1. Halve, pit, and peel the avocados. Cut the flesh into cubes.

2. Cut the strawberries into quarters.

3. Mix the avocados and strawberries together in a bowl with the lemon juice, and serve.

A daily intake of raw, fresh vegetables is an essential part of the Taoist diet.

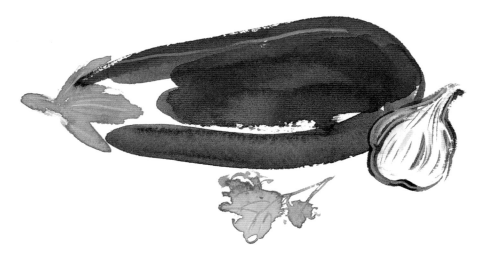

Baked Eggplant

A light summer dish that is ideal for vegans – and the rest of the family as well.

Vegan

Season:
Summer

Cooking time:
1½–1¾ hours
plus cooling
and chilling

4 eggplant (aubergines)

scant 1 cup/7 fl oz (200 ml) olive oil

1 lb (450 g) onions, peeled and chopped

3 cloves garlic, peeled and crushed

1 lb (450 g) fresh tomatoes, skinned and chopped

⅓ cup/4 tbsp (60 ml) chopped fresh parsley

salt and pepper to taste

1 tsp (5 ml) sugar

2 tbsp (30 ml) lemon juice

chopped parsley, to garnish

1. Slice the eggplant (aubergines) in half lengthwise and scoop out the fleshy middles.

2. Heat ¼ cup/3 tbsp (45 ml) olive oil in a skillet, add the onions and garlic, and fry gently for 5–10 minutes, or until the onions are soft but not brown.

3. Add the tomatoes, the ⅓ cup/4 tbsp (60 ml) parsley, and the flesh from the eggplant (aubergines). Season with salt and pepper to taste and simmer gently for 20–25 minutes, or until the liquid has reduced by half.

4. Spoon the tomato mixture into the hollowed-out eggplant (aubergine) halves. Place in a shallow ovenproof dish. Preheat the oven to 300°F, 150°C, gas mark 2.

5. Mix the rest of the oil with the sugar and lemon juice and ⅔ cup/¼ pint (150 ml) water. Add salt and pepper to taste and pour the mixture around the eggplant (aubergine) halves to keep them moist while they are cooking. Cook in the oven for about 1 hour.

6. After the eggplant (aubergines) are cooked, take them from the oven and leave them to cool for around 1 hour. Chill in the refrigerator for a further 2 hours at least. Serve cold, garnished with parsley.

Creamy Lima Beans

A wonderfully tasty side dish to accompany roast meat, or the beans could be served cold on their own.

Vegetarian

Season:
Summer

Cooking time:
25–35
minutes

4 tbsp/2 oz (50 g) butter

2 cloves garlic, peeled and chopped

4 shallots, peeled and chopped

1 lb (450 g) fresh baby lima (broad) beans, shelled

⅔ cup/¼ pint (150 ml) vegetable stock (see page 55)

scant 1 cup/7 fl oz (200 ml) heavy (double) cream

2 tbsp (30 ml) chopped chives

2 tbsp (30 ml) chopped parsley

grated zest of 1 lemon rind

salt and pepper to taste

1. Melt the butter in a skillet, add the garlic and shallots, and cook gently for about 5 minutes or until softened.

2. Add the beans and stock to the pan, bring to a boil, cover, and simmer for around 15 minutes, or until the beans are tender. Drain the pan, keeping the liquid as well as the vegetables.

3. Put the liquid in a blender and add ⅓ cup/ 4 tbsp (60 ml) of the beans. Blend to a smooth paste. Gradually add the cream and blend to make a smooth sauce.

4. Return the mixture to the skillet. Add the beans and herbs, and sprinkle the lemon zest on top. Add salt and pepper to taste, and reheat gently. Serve hot.

Baked Artichokes

A delicious vegan dish that can be served on its own or with rice. If you prefer, the artichokes can be grilled rather than baked.

Vegan

Season:
Summer

Cooking time:
45–55
minutes

4 large globe artichokes

½ cup/6 tbsp (90 ml) olive oil

salt and pepper to taste

lemon wedges, to garnish

1. Trim the artichokes of their stalks. Bring a large saucepan of water to a boil, add the artichokes, and simmer, covered, for 30 minutes or until you can easily pull a leaf away from the side of the artichoke. Drain.

2. Preheat the oven to 400°F, 200°C, gas mark 6.

3. Cut the artichokes in half lengthwise, remove the middles, and discard.

4. Place the artichoke halves, cut sides up, on a baking sheet. Pour a little olive oil into the hollowed-out middles and add salt and pepper to taste. Bake in the oven for about 20 minutes. Garnish with lemon wedges.

"Some prefer carrots, while others like cabbage"

Potato Salad

An ideal dish using seasonal new potatoes for a quick accompaniment to almost any summer meal.

Vegetarian

Season: Summer

Cooking time: 10–15 minutes plus cooling

2 lb (900 g) baby new potatoes

⅓ cup/4 tbsp (60 ml) Greek yogurt

⅓ cup/4 tbsp (60 ml) fresh mayonnaise

4 tsp (20 ml) whole grain mustard

1 tsp (5 ml) lemon juice

⅓ cup/4 tbsp (60 ml) chopped fresh dill

salt and pepper to taste

1. Scrub the new potatoes and cook in boiling water for 10–15 minutes, or until tender.
2. Meanwhile, mix all the other ingredients together, adding salt and pepper to taste.
3. Drain the potatoes and leave to cool for 5 minutes.
4. Pour the dressing over the potatoes and mix well. Serve while still warm, or leave to cool completely.

VARIATIONS

Try using chives, green onions, other fresh herbs, or garlic instead of dill.

Greek Salad

A traditional recipe for a Greek salad that can be served on its own or as an accompaniment to any summer dish.

Vegetarian

Season: Summer

Preparation time: 15–25 minutes

½ lb (225 g) tomatoes

½ large cucumber

¼ lb (100 g) feta cheese

1 onion, peeled and thinly sliced

½ cup/2 oz (50 g) pitted black olives

¼ cup/3 tbsp (45 ml) olive oil

1 tbsp (15 ml) lemon juice

2 tbsp (30 ml) chopped fresh herbs

pinch of sugar

salt and pepper to taste

chopped fresh herbs, to garnish

1. Cut the tomatoes into quarters and the cucumber and feta cheese into chunks.
2. Put the tomatoes and cucumber into a bowl with the onion and black olives and mix thoroughly.
3. Make a dressing of the olive oil, lemon juice, herbs, sugar, and salt and pepper to taste. Pour over the salad.
4. Sprinkle the chunks of feta cheese over the salad and garnish with fresh herbs.

Fresh Herb Salad

A very light, very yin, *very cooling salad for a hot day. This dish will appeal to those who like wandering meadows collecting wild flowers.*

Vegetarian

Season:
Summer

Cooking time:
15–25 minutes

8 large handfuls fresh herbs and edible flowers

1 tsp (5 ml) clear honey

2 tbsp (30 ml) lemon juice

2 tbsp (30 ml) olive oil

1 tbsp (15 ml) walnut oil

salt and pepper to taste

1. Prepare and wash enough fresh herbs and edible flowers for four people – sorrel, aragula (rocket), lamb's lettuce, chervil sprigs, dandelion, parsley sprigs, sweet violets, marigolds, etc.

2. Make a dressing by blending together the rest of the ingredients.

3. Pour the dressing over the salad vegetables and serve cold.

Nutty Coleslaw

A wonderfully cooling yin *salad to accompany summer recipes. This dish combines fruit and nuts, as well as salad vegetables.*

Vegetarian

Season:
Summer

Preparation time:
15–25 minutes

2 cups/½ lb (225 g) white cabbage, shredded

3 stalks celery, sliced

3 eating apples, peeled, cored, and thinly sliced

4 green onions (spring onions), sliced

¾ cup/2 oz (50 g) cashew nuts (or other nuts of your choice)

2 tbsp (30 ml) chopped parsley

⅔ cup/¼ pint (150 ml) fresh mayonnaise

2 tbsp (30 ml) Greek yogurt

1. Mix all the salad ingredients together in a large bowl.
2. Mix together the mayonnaise and yogurt, and pour over the salad. Mix thoroughly. Serve cold.

Parsnips with Lime

A delicious hot winter accompaniment to roasts and other meat dishes.

Vegetarian

Season:
Winter

Cooking time:
15–25 minutes

1½ lb (750 g) parsnips, peeled and sliced lengthwise

1 lime

4 tbsp/2 oz (50 g) butter

2 tbsp/1 oz (25 g) light muscovado sugar

thyme sprigs to garnish

1. Gently lower the parsnips into a saucepan of boiling water and cook for 5 minutes.
2. Pare the rind from the lime and cut into very thin shreds. Cut the lime in half and squeeze out the juice.
3. Melt the butter with the sugar in a large saucepan. Add the lime juice and heat very gently until all the sugar has dissolved.
4. Drain the parsnips and add to the lime and butter mixture. Cook over a moderate heat for about 10 minutes, or until golden brown.
5. Transfer to a serving dish and serve hot, garnished with sprigs of thyme and the shreds of lime rind.

Rosemary Roasted Potatoes

*A warming and traditional winter dish to accompany
any meat dish you are cooking.*

Vegan

Season:
Winter

Cooking time:
1¾–2 hours

2½ lb (1.1 kg) potatoes

2 sprigs rosemary

6 cloves garlic, peeled

¼ cup/3 tbsp (45 ml) olive oil

1. Preheat the oven to 400°F, 200°C, gas mark 6.
2. Peel the potatoes and cut into large chunks. Put in a large saucepan of cold water and bring to a boil, then reduce the heat and simmer for around 3 minutes. Drain the potatoes and leave to cool.
3. Strip the leaves off the rosemary sprigs. Put the potatoes in a large roasting pan and sprinkle with the rosemary leaves. Surround the potatoes with the garlic and pour the olive oil over them.
4. Roast in the oven for about 1½ hours, basting and turning a few times during cooking. Sprinkle with salt and pepper to taste, and serve hot.

Stuffed Peppers

*A tasty spring vegan recipe that can be served on its own
or as an accompaniment.*

Vegan

Season:
Spring

Cooking time:
55–65
minutes plus
chilling

4 sweet red peppers

a little oil, for brushing

¾ cup/6 oz (175 g) long-grain brown rice

8 tomatoes

8 green onions (spring onions), chopped

4 pitted black olives, chopped

½ cup/6 tbsp (90 ml) olive oil

2 tbsp (30 ml) white wine vinegar

1 large clove of garlic, peeled and crushed

salt and pepper to taste

1. Preheat the oven to 425°F, 220°C, gas mark 6.
2. Brush the peppers with oil, place on a baking sheet and bake in the oven for 15 minutes or until tender. Remove from the oven and leave to cool. When cool, halve the peppers lengthwise and remove the cores and seeds.
3. Cook the rice in boiling water for 40 minutes or until tender. Drain and rinse.
4. Chop the tomatoes and mix with the rice, green onions (spring onions), and olives.
5. Blend together the olive oil, vinegar, garlic, and salt and pepper to taste.
6. Spoon the rice mixture into the pepper halves and arrange on plates. Chill in the refrigerator for around 30 minutes before serving.

"Never
do anything
standing that
you can do
sitting, or
anything
sitting that
you can do
lying down"

THE TAO OF PUDDINGS AND DESSERTS

Puddings and Desserts

Traditionally, puddings and desserts have been a way of providing a little *yin* treat at the end of a meal to cleanse the palate and to clear the mouth of any residual *yang* taste.

The *Yin* of Puddings

Puddings and desserts are, by their very nature *yin*, as they are invariably sweet or made from fruit of some sort. Sweet treats taken at the end of a meal satisfy our need for sweet tastes but shouldn't be eaten between meals as they can dull our appetite. Picking at food, especially sweet *yin* foods, between meals, is a sure way to put on weight, as your digestive system doesn't have a chance to rest, nor do you ever allow yourself to feel hungry.

Remember the Peach

A peach, fresh picked from the tree and still warm with *yang* sunshine, is probably the best dessert of all, but a little fresh fruit at the end of any meal is refreshing as well as good oral hygiene. Try to keep puddings and sweets simple.

When to Eat Puddings

In the winter, a hot pudding is a good idea as it warms the stomach and generates internal *yang* heat, which is exactly what we want. In the summer, cold puddings are best as they preserve the internal *yin* coolness which, again, is just what we want.

Obviously, if you live in a cold or moderate climate you will need more hot food than if you live in a very warm climate. Hot puddings are best made with fruit that can be washed; then boiled or steamed quickly, and served with a little fresh cream or yogurt. There is not always any need to add further sugar as puddings are not meant to be overly sweet.

Any pastry you use in your puddings should be kept to a minimum. Although flour made from wheat has quite a good *yin/yang* balance, it can reduce the *yin* qualities in some puddings. Ice creams should be made at home rather than shop-bought. If you do buy any, check the ingredients and make sure that what you are buying is actually made from cream and not vegetable fats. Fruit sorbets are very refreshing on a summer's day and can be easily made with fresh fruit and lots of ice.

Try to include as much fresh fruit as possible in your diet. It can be served as an appealing dessert with careful presentation.

Blackberry and Oatmeal Cream

Ideally, the blackberries for this dish should be picked fresh the day you make it.

Season:
Fall

Preparation time:
10–15 minutes

⅔ cup/2 oz (50 g) coarse oatmeal

2½ cups/1 pint (600 ml) fresh heavy (double) cream

¼ cup/2 oz (50 g) superfine (caster) sugar

1 cup/¼ lb (100 g) fresh blackberries

1. Put the oatmeal into a saucepan and shake it over a high heat for a minute to crisp it.
2. Whip the heavy (double) cream until it is thick, then fold in the sugar, oatmeal, and most of the blackberries.
3. Decorate with the remaining blackberries before serving.

Poached Apricots with Pears

A delicious fall pudding to follow a lightish lunch, very filling.

Season:
Fall

Preparation time:
15–20 minutes

2 tbsp/1 oz (25 g) butter

2 tbsp/1 oz (25 g) soft brown sugar

1 tbsp (15 ml) lemon juice

1½ lb (750 g) apricots, pitted and sliced

1½ lb (750 g) ripe pears, peeled, cored, and sliced

1 tbsp (15 ml) brandy

1. Put the butter, sugar, and lemon juice in a saucepan with ⅔ cup/¼ pint (150 ml) water and warm gently to dissolve the sugar.
2. Cut the apricots into quarters and the pears into chunks.
3. Pour the syrup over the fruit, then return to the saucepan and simmer for 10 minutes or until the pears are tender.
4. Stir in the brandy and serve hot.

Honey Rice Pudding

This is very filling and warming on a cold fall day.
However much you make, it simply won't be enough.

Season:
Fall

Cooking time:
2½–3 hours

2½ cups/1 pint (600 ml) milk

1¼ cups/½ pint (300 ml) half-and-half (single cream)

⅓ cup/3 oz (75 g) pudding rice

2 tbsp/1 oz (25 g) butter

2 tbsp (30 ml) superfine (caster) sugar

¼ tsp (1.25 ml) grated nutmeg

¼ tsp (1.25 ml) ground cinnamon

⅓ cup/2 oz (50 g) flaked almonds

¼ cup/3 tbsp (45 ml) clear honey

1 tbsp (15 ml) lemon juice

1. Preheat the oven to 300°F, 150°C, gas mark 2.

2. Mix together all the ingredients, except the lemon juice, nuts, and honey, and put into an ovenproof dish. Bake for 2½–3 hours or until lightly set and golden brown on top.

3. Sprinkle the flaked almonds over the top of the pudding. Mix together the honey and lemon juice, and pour over the nutty top.

4. Place under a hot broiler until the entire topping is golden brown. Serve hot or cold.

> "One should be just as careful in choosing one's pleasures as in avoiding calamities"

Caramel Pineapple

An unusual and delicious pudding, just right for a spring dessert when you need a taste of the exotic.

Season:
Spring

Cooking time:
45–55 minutes

1 good-sized pineapple, about 2 lb (900 g)

2 tbsp (30 ml) clear honey

½ cup/6 tbsp (90 ml) brandy

heavy (double) cream, to serve

1. Preheat the oven to 375°F, 190°C, gas mark 5.
2. Trim the leaves off the pineapple and cut the fruit lengthwise into quarters. Cut the flesh away from the skin but leave it in place. Score across the flesh to cut the sections into chunks.
3. Put the pineapple in an ovenproof dish and spoon the honey over it. Cook in the oven for around 45 minutes, basting occasionally, until golden brown.
4. Heat the brandy gently in a saucepan, pour it over the pineapple, and ignite. When the flames have gone out, pour the juices over it. Serve hot with heavy (double) cream.

Sticky Fudge Pudding

Nothing in moderation — this one's for serious pudding-lovers.

Season:
Winter

Cooking time:
55–65 minutes

1 stick plus 2 tbsp/5 oz (150 g) butter, softened

¾ cup/6 oz (175 g) light brown sugar

1¼ cups/½ pint (300 ml) heavy (double) cream

1 egg

1 cup/¼ lb (100 g) self-raising flour

½ cup/2 oz (50 g) walnuts, chopped

1. Preheat the oven to 350°F, 180°C, gas mark 4. Grease a deep baking dish.
2. Warm half the butter and ½ cup/¼ lb (100 g) of the sugar in a small saucepan with the cream. Boil the mixture for around 3 minutes, then pour a little into the baking dish to cover the bottom.
3. Beat the egg. Beat in the remaining sugar with the rest of the butter until light and fluffy, then stir in the flour and nuts. Pour into the baking dish and bake in the oven for about 50 minutes or until just firm.
4. Turn the pudding out on to a serving dish. Warm the remainder of the fudge sauce and pour over the pudding.

Toffee Apple Pudding

A simply delicious traditional fall pudding that children adore – and it will tempt sweet-toothed adults too.

Season:
Fall

Cooking time:
10–20 minutes

1 large eating apple, peeled, cored, and chopped

1 medium cooking apple, peeled, cored, and chopped

¼ cup/2 oz (50 g) demerara sugar

4 tbsp/2 oz (50 g) butter

juice of ½ lemon

2 pieces wholegrain bread, cubed

⅓ cup/4 tbsp (60 ml) heavy (double) cream, whipped

1. Sprinkle the apples with the sugar. Melt half the butter in a frying pan, add the apples and fry quickly until just soft. Turn out into a serving dish, sprinkle with the lemon juice and keep warm.
2. Melt the remaining butter in the frying pan with the juices remaining, and add the bread cubes. Fry until crisp and brown.
3. Add to the apples and mix well. Serve hot with a topping of whipped cream.

Baked Bananas

A simple, but deliciously sweet and sticky hot winter pudding to warm cold people.

 Season:
Winter

Cooking time:
40–50 minutes

4 tbsp/2 oz (50 g) butter

2 tbsp (30 ml) light brown soft sugar

2 tbsp (30 ml) lemon juice

4 bananas

2 tbsp (30 ml) brandy

half-and-half (single cream), to serve

1. Preheat the oven to 350°F, 180°C, gas mark 4.
2. Put the butter, sugar, and lemon juice into a shallow casserole and place in the oven for a few minutes, until everything has melted.
3. Peel the bananas and cut each in half lengthwise. Arrange in the casserole and spoon over the liquid. Add the brandy and cover the dish. Return to the oven and cook for 30 minutes or so.
4. Serve hot with half-and-half (single cream).

Fruit Salad

A delicious light summer yin pudding that is ideal for vegans and full of vitamins and goodness.

Vegan

Season:
Summer

Cooking time:
5 minutes
plus chilling

2 tbsp (30 ml) soft brown sugar

grated zest and juice of 1 lemon

1 large dessert apple, cored and quartered

1 large pear, peeled, cored, and quartered

1 banana, peeled

1 small pineapple

2 oranges

¼ lb (100 g) green grapes

¼ lb (100 g) wild strawberries, hulled and sliced

1. Put the sugar and lemon zest into a small saucepan with ½ cup/6 tbsp (90 ml) water, and bring to a boil. Reduce the heat and simmer for about 2 minutes, then strain and leave to cool. Stir in the lemon juice.
2. Slice the apple, pear, and banana into a bowl and pour the liquid over it. Mix well until all the fruit is coated.
3. Peel the pineapple and cut the flesh into chunks. Peel the oranges and cut into chunks.
4. Add the pineapple and oranges to the bowl with the grapes and strawberries. Mix well. Spoon out into individual dishes and chill in the refrigerator. Serve cold.

Red Berry Compote

*A quick and simple but delicious summer pudding to go with a
picnic, or for an elegant lunch on the lawn.*

 Season:
Summer

Cooking time:
5–10 minutes
plus cooling
and chilling

¼ cup/2 oz (50 g) soft brown
sugar

1 cup/½ lb (225 g) black
currants

1 lb (450 g) red currants

grated zest and juice
of 1 orange

2 tbsp (30 ml) clear honey

¾ lb (350 g) strawberries

1. Put the sugar in a small saucepan with
   about ⅔ cup/¼ pint (150 ml) water and heat
   gently until the sugar has dissolved. Bring
   to a boil and let it bubble for about
   1 minute.

2. Add the black currants, and red currants,
   and grated orange zest to the pan and
   simmer for about 1 minute, or until the fruit
   is just soft. Remove from the heat and stir in
   the honey. Leave to cool.

3. Stir the orange juice into the fruit and
   transfer to a serving bowl. Cover and
   chill well.

4. Just before serving, thinly slice the
   strawberries and add them to the bowl.

"When you have
only two pennies
left in the world,
buy a loaf of
bread with one,
and a lily with
the other"

SAUCES

Sauces are meant to be light and to complement a dish, not heavy and smothering. Most sauces are by the nature of their ingredients fairly *yin*, although cheese and egg sauces will be more *yang* because of the animal products they contain.

When do You Need Sauces?

If you are serving fairly heavily *yang* meats, then a light *yin* sauce to counteract the energy imbalance would be a good idea. A light sauce made from fruit is always an easy *yin* addition to a dish, whereas cheese or egg sauces would be too heavy. Use the cheese and egg sauces as a *yang* complement to *yin* dishes such as cauliflower.

Hot Spicy Sauces

Use hot spicy sauces to redress any *yang* imbalance. These can be made from a basic béchamel sauce with various herbs added to flavor them as you require.

The basic question to ask when you are cooking and not sure whether you need a sauce is "What will it do for this dish?" If you use sauces to add flavor, then why isn't the flavor there in the first place? Sauces should complement, not take over. They should redress any *yin/yang* imbalance and they should be light and barely noticeable.

It is best to avoid shop-bought sauces, especially those such as tomato sauce which is full of sugar and might get used far too frequently. If you need a tomato sauce, it is probably best to make your own and then you know that it is fresh.

A classic sauce like hollandaise is a very well-balanced sauce as the vinegar balances out the *yang*-ness of the egg yolks and butter. You can serve hollandaise with anything from fish to asparagus, lamb to broccoli. If you want the hollandaise sauce to be a little less *yin* and slightly more *yang*, then add lemon juice instead of vinegar.

Dressings aren't really sauces but are often added to salads. They are usually very *yin* in their effect owing to the vinegar they usually contain, but you can make them a little less so by substituting lemon juice.

Sauces and dressings should always be offered to your guests to add to their own food rather than be added by you. That way they can decide if they want or need any.

Sauces include a lot of different ingredients and can be fiddly to make in your own home – especially when there are so many varieties in the stores; but home-made sauces are absolutely delicious.

OIL

There really is only one oil to use when you are cooking and that is olive oil. It is versatile, efficient, healthy, and flavorsome. You can use it for cooking, to add to dressings, even as a skin lotion to keep your skin wrinkle-free and smooth.

What Sort of Olive Oil?

The name "olive oil" is as vague as saying "wine." You need to know a little more before choosing what sort of olive oil you want to use. There are at least 700 cultivated varieties of olive tree (*olea europaea*), and each produces its own sort of fruit. The best oil producers blend their fruit to produce a distinctive and unique flavor, but even that is not a dependable factor because the seasons change, there may be more rain one year and the fruit tastes different from month to month. The oil even changes flavor depending on its storage conditions.

Buy Fresh

Olive oil should be bought as fresh as you need it; unlike wine, which improves with age, olive oil does go off quite quickly. It loses its flavor if you chill it so don't keep it in the refrigerator. "First press" and "cold press" refer to the processes whereby oil is freshly squeezed. These oils are known as virgin, or even extra-virgin if the oil is of the very highest quality.

Second press oil is produced when olives that have already been squeezed once to make virgin oil are squeezed again. This oil has a little high-quality oil added to it to make it taste better. Second press oil – often sold as "pure" oil – is not of such high quality and can be used for cooking.

Olive Trees

Olive oil is good for you and provides all the goodness you need in cooking. The fruits come from a very *yin* tree indeed. The olive tree takes a long time to come to fruit and it is no coincidence that the olive branch is an international symbol of peace. You cannot have peace unless you have the time and patience to tend your olive trees, and the warmth, sunshine, and peace is conveyed to us in the oil.

Other Oils

If you prefer not to use olive oil, walnut and sunflower seed oils are also very good as they are light enough to cook with and can be used in dressings.

"Be as pure as the orange and you will live forever"

SPICES

Spices, as plants, are *yin*, but the more aromatic they are the more *yang* they become. The sweeter they are the more *yin* they are. For instance, chilies are quite *yang* while licorice is quite *yin*. You can use the sweeter spices in cooling *yin* recipes and the aromatic *yang* spices in warming *yang* dishes.

Spice Myth

There is a common myth about spices: they were originally used to flavor meat that wasn't as fresh as it might have been, or to flavor poor-quality meat. This simply is not true. Spices have been used as long as humans have been preparing food. They add flavor, excitement, variety, and delicious aromas to our food. Confucius himself said that food wasn't proper food without the addition of spices.

Choosing spices is a matter of taste and preference. Try choosing just one spice to add to a dish to allow that flavor to be savored. Too many cooks spoil their meals by adding too many spices so that they blur and the tastes become indistinct. You need to be discriminating and selective so that your guests can appreciate the delicate flavor of the chosen spice without it being swamped.

Warming Yang Spices

Some spices are very hot indeed and their warming *yang* properties can be overpowering. No one should be forced to eat food that is too spicy and you should err on the side of caution when using the hotter spices.

Cooling Yin Spices

Sweeter spices, such as vanilla, licorice, and nutmeg, can be used to flavor summer puddings and sweets, but again they should be used with a light touch to provide delicate flavors and subtle tastes rather than swamping the food.

If you heat sweet spices you change them from *yin* to *yang*; spices like cinnamon would have a more warming *yang* aspect if used in mulled wine and drunk to combat the winter cold.

Likewise, *yang* spices used in cold dishes, such as cold curried eggs and rice, become more *yin* and can be quite cooling and refreshing on a summer's day if they are eaten as part of a picnic on the lawn.

Licorice Root

Cayenne Pepper

Paprika

Cloves

Nutmeg

Cinnamon Bark

Cumin

Star Anise

Coriander

Vanilla

black

white

green

Pepper

Juniper

DRINKS

Any liquid is, by its nature, *yin*, as are drinks, no matter what they are. Water is the most *yin* and probably the most ideal for us to drink. However, we need pleasure, flavor, and variety so we should feel free to enjoy any drink we want just as long as its effect is beneficial.

Alcohol

Alcohol is a very *yin* drink, and an excessive intake of alcohol of any sort will cause us to have a *yin* surplus and that's why we get drunk. You may notice that people who drink a lot often go for very *yang* foods, such as salty crisps and peanuts, to try to counteract this. Spirits are more *yang* than wines, which are made from fruit, and white wines more *yang* than red ones.

Coffee and Tea

Coffee and tea are both very *yin* and can have a detrimental *yin* effect if drunk to excess. They both become less *yin* if you add *yang* milk to them.

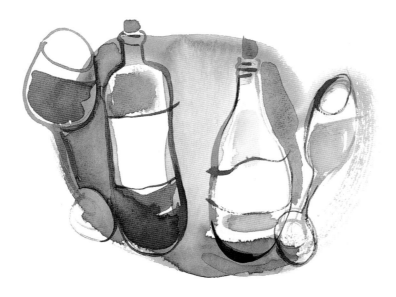

Fruit Juices

Fruit juices are very *yin* and are traditionally drunk first thing in the morning to counteract the *yang* effect of a predominantly meat breakfast such as bacon and eggs. Nowadays people tend to go for more *yin* breakfasts such as museli and cereals but still drink the fruit juice as well. Mid-morning you may find yourself hungry because your system has become too *yin* and needs a little *yang* to help it along.

Hot and Cold Drinks

Hot drinks are more *yang* in their aspect, which is why we tend to drink more mulled wines, soups, and hot chocolate in the winter to warm us up and keep the cold out. Fizzy drinks are more *yang* than still ones. Pale drinks are more *yang* than dark ones. The sweeter the drink the more *yin* it is.

Seeking a Balance

As in all things, we are seeking a balance between *yin* and *yang*, and you should be aware of the *yin* effect of too much liquid. Likewise, too little liquid is too *yang* for your system.

Try to balance what you provide for your guests as well: serve the more *yang* drinks such as white wine with more *yin* dishes such as fish and vegetables, and the more *yin* drinks such as red wine with the more *yang* dishes such as red meat. It is traditional to have a *yang* spirit such as a brandy at the end of the meal to counteract the effect of the *yin* pudding.

"If you are one with nature, you share nature's fruits"

THE TAO OF FOOD AND HAPPINESS

We all want to be happy and we all want to live our lives in the best possible way. It makes sense to combine our eating habits with our pursuit of happiness so that we eat to improve our health and longevity as well as putting us firmly in balance with both the Tao and ourselves. If we are what we eat then it makes sense to incorporate Taoist principles into our eating patterns so we can benefit from the wisdom of so many who have gone before us and explored the interaction of food and happiness.

Use Taoist Principles

What we eat provides us with energy – *ch'i* – and that energy empowers us and brings us life. That energy should be both healthy and alive. If we eat dead energy we will feel sluggish and stagnant. Choose the freshest ingredients you can afford. The farther food is from its natural growth cycle, the more we should be wary of it and reject it.

Understand the Tao

There is a movement and pattern in all things. Eat cool food in the summer; eat warm food in the winter. Eat less when you are inactive; eat more when you are physically busy. Try not to eat foods which are extreme – very spicy or very sweet or very meaty. Try to achieve balance in your diet so that both *yin* and *yang* energies are eaten. However if you are predominantly *yang* then eat more *yin* food, and if you are mainly *yin* then eat more *yang* food.

Be Responsible

Don't waste food and don't eat more than is good for you or more than you want. Try to grow as much of your food as possible if you have a garden. Be discriminating in your choice of meat – consider how it is reared and prepared. If you are planning a garden try to plant fruit trees and a vegetable patch to maximize your potential for home-grown produce.

Yin and Yang

There is a balance of these in everything. We may not see them both but they are always there. The more comfortable our lives become the greater the cost in terms of world pollution. The more we rely on modern medicine the greater our need for stronger medications. The quicker food is to prepare and eat, the worse our health becomes from poor diet.

Put Something Back

Plant the occasional seed so that others may benefit. This may be the seed of an apple so it will grow and others may have fruit; or it may be the seed of an idea so that others may be intrigued to find out more; or even the seed of your own good health so others may be inspired.

INDEX

A
almond soup 61
apple rice 87
artichokes
   baked 105
   and Brussels sprout purée 99
asparagus and almond soup 62
avocado
   soup 58
   and strawberry salad 102

B
beef broth 69
beet salad 100
bouquet garni 55

C
carrots
   and celeriac soup 59
   in orange sauce 100
   and parsnip au gratin 101
celery, bean, and onion stew 98
cheese 16
   and fish pie 77
   and rice soufflé 91
chicken
   and apple casserole 70
   and coconut soup 60
   grilled salad 72
   risotto 89
   soup 56, 62
   stock 55
   and zucchini stir-fry 70

D
duck salad with beans 73

E
eggplant, baked 104

F
feng shui 18–21, 36
Fire 24–26

F (cont.)
fish 15, 75–82
flounder Veronique 82
fried rice 86
fried rice rissoles 92
fruit and nut risotto 89

G
ginger squash 101
Greek salad 106

H
healing foods 22–23
herb salad 107

K
karma 39–41

L
lamb with yogurt 68
lemon rice 88
lima beans 105
liver with orange 68
lobster, grilled 80

M
mackerel, cider baked 78
meat 15, 42, 48, 65–73
meditation 34–36
Metal 24–26
monkfish with bacon 82
mushrooms
   and nut risotto 91
   and rice pancakes 93

N
nutty coleslaw 108
nutty rice salad 94
orange and cucumber soup 58

P
parsnips with lime 108
peach 10, 110
peppers, stuffed 109
pork and bacon sausages 66
pork chops with plums 66

P (cont.)
pork and parsnip bake 67
potatoes
   and prawn salad 81
   rosemary roasted 109
   salad 106
prawn and potato salad 81
puddings 110–17

R
rice 16, 28–9, 84–94
rice cakes 94
root vegetable casserole 98

S
salads 96–109
salmon
   roasted with mustard 79
   and spinach pasta 76
salsify lemon soup 61
sorrel, potato, and rice soup 63
soups 56–63
spicy rice 88

T
trout and lentils 76
tuna steaks with basil butter 80

V
vegetable pilau rice 92
vegetable stock 55
vegetables 96–109
vegetarianism/veganism 39,
   42–3

W
Water 24–26
Wood 24–26

Y
yin and *yang* 14–16, 19–24, 28,
   30–3, 40, 42–3, 46, 48, 75,
   96–97, 110

Z
zucchini salad 102

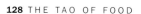